Programming in C: A Modern Approach

Dr.P. Prabu

Dr.T. Senthilnathan

Dr.R. Sivakumar

Published by

BONFRING®
Intellectual Integrity

Programming in C: A Modern Approach

9 789386 638724 >

ISBN 978-93-86638-72-4

Authors

Dr.P. Prabu

Dr.T. Senthilnathan

Dr.R. Sivakumar

Bonfring

309, 2nd Floor, 5th Street Extension, Gandhipuram,

Coimbatore-641 012.

Tamilnadu, India.

E-mail: info@bonfring.org

Website: www.bonfring.org

Phone: 0422 4213231

Acknowledgement

First of all we would like to thank supreme power almighty God who is obviously is the source of life, strength of knowledge and wisdom.

We would like to express our gratitude to the many people who saw us through this book; to all those who provided support, talked things over, read, wrote, offered comments, allowed us to quote their remarks and assisted in the editing, proofreading and design.

It is pleasure to mention our special thanks to the management of CHRIST (Deemed to be University), Bangalore for the academic support and the facilities provided to complete this book.

We would like to particularly thank Professor Joy Paulose, Head, Department of Computer Science, who have been always helping and encouraging throughout this work.

Also, we extend our sincere thanks to all teaching and non-teaching staff members of the Computer Science Department for their extensive support throughout our text book work.

We would like to thank our family for standing beside us throughout our career and writing this book. Their motivation continued us to improve our knowledge towards the development of our career.

Finally, our sincere thanks to the Publisher, for their help and co-operation in publishing this book.

Chapters	Contents	Page No

CHAPTER 1

INTRODUCTION TO PROGRAMMING

1.1. What is Program?

A program is a sequence of instructions that tell a computer how to do a task. When a computer follows the instructions in a program, we say it *executes* the program. You can think of it like a recipe that tells you how to make a peanut butter sandwich. In this model, you are the computer, making a sandwich is the task, and the recipe is the program that tells you how to execute the task.

- Activity: Come up with a sequence of instructions to tell someone how to make a peanut butter sandwich. Don't leave any steps out, or put them in the wrong order.

Was that easy? Did you remember all the steps? Maybe you forgot to tell me to use a knife to spread the peanut butter. Now I've got peanut butter all over my hands! Of course, you say, a person wouldn't be that dumb. But a computer *is* that dumb. A computer will only do what you tell it to do. This might make programming frustrating at first, but it's relieving in a way: if you do everything right, you know exactly what the computer is going to do, because you told it.

Of course, computers don't understand recipes written on paper. Computers are machines, and at the most basic level, they are a collection of switches—where 1 represents "on" and 0 represents "off". Everything that a computer does is implemented in this most basic of all numbering systems—*binary*. If you really wanted to tell a computer what to do directly, you'd have to talk to it in *binary*, giving it coded sequences of 1s and 0s that tell it which instructions to execute. However, this is nearly impossible. In practice, we use a *programming language*.

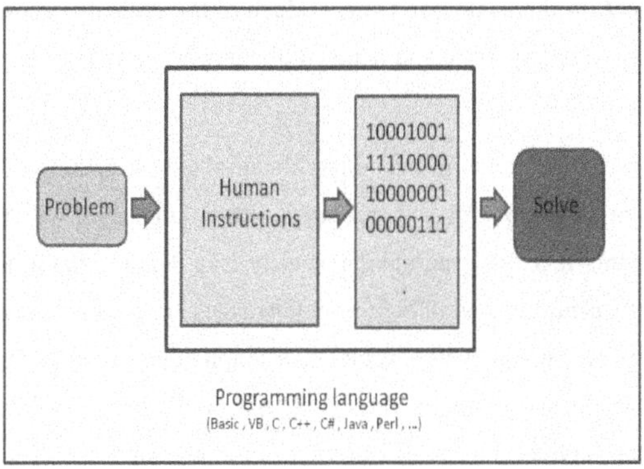

Algorithm and Flowchart for Solving Problem

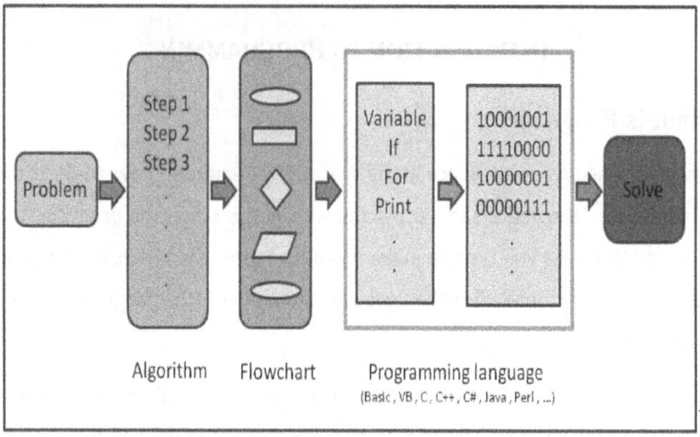

1.2. Programming Languages

The purpose of programming is to tell the computer what to do. Computers are better at doing some things than you are, like a chef is better at cooking than you are. It's easier to tell a chef to cook you a meal than to cook it yourself. The more precise you are in your request, the more your meal will turn out how you like it. In most scenarios like this in real life, small amounts of ambiguity and misinterpretation are acceptable. Perhaps the chef will boil your potato before mashing it instead of baking it. With computers, however, ambiguity is rarely acceptable. Programs are so complex that if the computer just guessed at the meaning of ambiguous or vague requests, it might cause problems so subtle that you'd never find them. Programming languages, therefore, have been designed to accept only completely clear and unambiguous statements. The program might still have problems, but the blame is then squarely on you, not on the computer's guess. Much of the difficulty in programming comes from having to be perfectly precise and detailed about everything instead of just giving high-level producers.

Some languages require total and complete detail about everything. C and C++ are such languages, and are called ***low-level languages***. Other languages will make all sorts of assumptions, and this lets the programmer specify less detail. Python and Basic are such languages, and are called. In general, high-level languages are easier to program but give you less control. Control is sometimes important, for example if you want your program to run as quickly as possible. Most of the time total control and speed aren't necessary, and as computers get faster high-level languages become more popular. Here we will deal exclusively with high-level languages. Low-level languages are generally similar except there's often more lines of code to write to accomplish the same thing.

Statements

Most programming languages have the concept of a statement. A ***statement*** is a command that the programmer gives to the computer. For example:

```
print "Hi there!"
```

This command has a verb ("print") and other details (what to print). In this case, the command print means "show on the screen," not "print on the printer." The programmer either gives the statement directly to the computer (by typing it while running a special program), or creates a text file with the command in it. You could create a file called "hi.txt" using a program like Notepad, put the above command in it, and give the file to the computer. (The details of how to do all this are language- and system-specific, so they won't be covered here. This is just an introduction to the concepts.)

If you have more than one command in the file, each will be performed in order, top to bottom. So the file could contain:

```
print "Hi there!"
print "Strange things are afoot..."
```

The computer will perform each of these commands sequentially. It's invaluable to be able to "play computer" when programming. Ask yourself, "If I were the computer, what would I do with these statements?" If you're not sure what the answer is, then you are very likely to write incorrect programs. Stop and check the manual for the programming language you're using.

In the above case, the computer will look at the first statement, determine that it's a print statement, look at what needs to be printed, and display that text on the computer screen. It'll look like this:

```
Hi there!
```

Note that the quotation marks aren't there. Their purpose in the program is to tell the computer where the text begins and ends, just like in English prose. The computer will then continue to the next statement, perform its command, and the screen will look like this:

```
Hi there!
Strange things are afoot...
```

When the computer gets to the end of the text file, it stops and waits for further instructions. There are many different kinds of statements, depending on which programming language is being used. For example, there could be a beep statement that causes the computer to output a beep on its speaker, or a window statement that causes a new window to pop up.

Also, the way statements are written will vary depending on the programming language. The programming language Python uses statements that look like the above. In C you would write:

```
puts("Hi there!");
puts("Strange things are afoot...");
```

Note a few differences:

1. The parameters (the text in quotation marks that print uses to determine what to display) are surrounded by parentheses.
2. Each statement is terminated by a semicolon.
3. The verb print is called puts, for "put string". The word ***string*** is the computer term for some text. It comes from "a string of letters." The "put" means "put on the screen."

These differences are fairly superficial. The set of rules like the first two is called a programming language's ***syntax***. The set of verbs is called its ***library***.

Syntax

All computer languages have syntax, rules to create proper statements, just like natural languages do. For example, most sentences are ended with a full stop or a period. Likewise it is common for statements in source code to be ended with a semicolon, but many languages do not have this requirement so it is important to know the syntax of the language you are programming in. For example, if you wanted the computer to display two different things you could write:

```
print "I have a dog.  His name is Bort."
```

or you could write:

```
print "I have a dog.  " + "His name is Bort."
```

The second example has two strings, each enclosed in quotation marks. There's a plus (+) sign in between them, which means, "Attach the two strings together, turning them into a single string." (Attaching two strings is called ***concatenation***.) The two above statements will display the same thing:

I have a dog. His name is Bort.

In the above examples there's no reason why you'd use a + and two strings when you could just use a single string, as in the first example, but below there will be cases where concatenation of strings is necessary. The languages Python and Java use plus (+) for string concatenation, Perl and PHP use the period (.), and Visual Basic uses ampersand (&). Again, these differences are superficial; what's important is the concept of string concatenation and of language syntax to do things like concatenation. Separate in your mind an underlying concept and a particular language's way of expressing that concept.

When programs are compiled, or converted into an executable program, they are analyzed by a parser, the equivalent of a proofreader, to determine if the syntax is correct. Assuming the program's source code is syntactically correct, the compiler will continue to analyze the source code to determine if there are any semantical errors.

Semantics refers to the meaning or logic of a computer program. Two syntactically correct statements can make perfect sense by themselves, but they may not make sense when placed next to each other. Sometimes these flaws in logic can be detected by the compiler, what is known as a compile-time error, but typically these errors surface when the program is executed, known as run-time errors.

Observe the following conversation:

Alice: Terrible news. Carl's wife was in a car accident.

Bob: Oh, that is terrible. Send some nice flowers and get everyone to sign a card.

Alice: Sure. Oh, and Dan called in sick again.

Bob: Not again. Send him a pink slip.

The conversation makes perfect, logical sense. This conversation shows a good, consistent use of semantics.

Now observe this conversation:

Alice: Terrible news. Carl's wife was in a car accident.

Bob: Not again. Send him a pink slip.

Alice: Sure. Oh, and Dan called in sick again.

Bob: Oh, that is terrible. Send some nice flowers and get everyone to sign a card.

Although this conversation contains the exact same sentences as the previous one, it has a very different meaning. A human may be able to bend the rules of grammar and structure to determine the intended meaning of a conversation, but computers are not as flexible. Therefore, it is important to use proper syntax and use good semantics in order to properly convey to the computer what you want it to do. Understand though, that the first conversation could have been rearranged and still have the same meaning or different sentences could have been used to convey the same idea. In that sense there can be many different ways to write the same program.

1.3. Compilation vs Interpretation

A compiled program has to be modified into machine code before it is used. The binary is then permanently stored. As an analogy, think of a novel that was written in one language and then translated into another.

For example, the Harry Potter novels were written in British English, and were then subsequently translated into 67 other languages, including Hindi, Latvian, and Latin. In much the same way, a computer program can be compiled (or "translated") into machine code, and it may potentially be compiled into different architectures (or "dialects") of machine code to suit different computers. Each translation will be a unique version of the program, in the same way that each translated book is a unique version of the original novel. To take the analogy further, if I was fortunate enough to have written the first Harry Potter novel, it may be the case that I wouldn't understand the language into which it is translated. Thus I could be given the Latvian version of the novel, and I could reasonably surmise that it tells the same story as the British English one, but I would be unable to read it. In the same sense, the version of my program that has been compiled into machine code might be impossible for me to read: it is said to be "machine-readable", in that the computer can understand it, but it is far from easily readable for humans.

An interpreted program is stored in a human-readable form. When the program is executed, an interpreter modifies the human-readable content as it is run. This is analogous to the role that a human interpreter performs. For example, rather than translating the British English version of Harry Potter into Latvian and then providing the Latvian version to someone who understands the language, (as per compilation), we could hire a translator who knows both British English and Latvian. The translator may choose to read each line from the British English novel, translate each line (one at a time) into Latvian, and, as each line is translated, relate it to the listener. The computer interpreter performs the same function: it reads an instruction in one programming language, translates it into machine code, and then executes the machine code version. Once that instruction is out of the way it moves along to the next, performing exactly the same task, in much the same way that the interpreter of the Harry Potter novel would move on to the next line once the first has been related. Unlike compiled programs, at no point is a complete, discrete, machine code version of the program produced: at any point in time only a small number of instructions exist as machine code versions, and these will be removed from the computer's memory when they are no longer required.

There are advantages for both types of software development. As a generalization, compiled programs are faster to run but slower to develop. Compiled programs often run faster because the computer only needs to execute the previously translated instructions. In interpreted languages, every time the program is run the computer also needs to translate each of the instructions. This translation causes a delay, slowing the execution of the program. On the other hand, interpreted languages are often written in a smaller time frame, because the languages are simpler and the whole program does not need to be compiled each time a new feature is bug tested.

1.4. Importance of Algorithm

The first step towards an understanding of why the study and knowledge of algorithms are so important is to define exactly what we mean by an algorithm. According to the popular algorithms textbook Introduction to Algorithms (Second Edition by **Thomas H. Cormen, Charles E. Leiserson, Ronald L. Rivest, Clifford Stein**), **"an algorithm is any well-defined computational procedure that takes some value, or set of values, as input and produces some value, or set of values as output.**" In other words, algorithms are like road maps for accomplishing a given, well-defined task. So, a chunk of code that calculates the terms of the Fibonacci sequence is an implementation of a particular algorithm. Even a simple function for adding two numbers is an algorithm in a sense, albeit a simple one.

Some algorithms, like those that compute the Fibonacci sequences, are intuitive and may be innately embedded into our logical thinking and problem solving skills. However, for most of us, complex algorithms are best studied so we can use them as building blocks for more efficient logical problem solving in the future. In fact, you may be surprised to learn just how many complex algorithms people use every day when they check their e-mail or listen to music on their computers. This article will introduce some basic ideas related to the analysis of algorithms, and then put these into practice with a few examples illustrating why it is important to know about algorithms.

One of the most important aspects of an algorithm is how fast it is. It is often easy to come up with an algorithm to solve a problem, but if the algorithm is too slow, it's back to the drawing board. Since the exact speed of an algorithm depends on where the algorithm is run, as well as the exact details of its implementation, computer scientists typically talk about the runtime relative to the size of the input. For example, if the input consists of N integers, an algorithm might have a runtime proportional to N2, represented as O(N2). This means that if you were to run an implementation of the algorithm on your computer with an input of size N, it would take C*N2 seconds, where C is some constant that doesn't change with the size of the input.

However, the execution time of many complex algorithms can vary due to factors other than the size of the input. For example, a sorting algorithm may run much faster when given a set of integers that are already sorted than it would when given the same set of integers in a random order. As a result, you often hear people talk about the worst-case runtime, or the average-case runtime. The worst-case runtime is how long it would take for the algorithm to run if it were given the most insidious of all possible inputs. The average-case runtime is the average of how long it would take the algorithm to run if it were given all possible inputs. Of the two, the worst-case is often easier to reason about, and therefore is more frequently used as a benchmark for a given algorithm. The process of determining the worst-case and average-case runtimes for a given algorithm can be tricky, since it is usually impossible to run an algorithm on all possible inputs. There are many good online resources that can help you in estimating these values.

1.5. Pseudocode

Pseudocode (pronounced SOO-doh-kohd) is a detailed yet readable description of what a computer program or algorithm must do, expressed in a formally-styled natural language rather than in a programming language. Pseudocode is sometimes used as a detailed step in the process of developing a program. It allows designers or lead programmers to express the design in great detail and provides programmers a detailed template for the next step of writing code in a specific programming language.

Because pseudocode is detailed yet readable, it can be inspected by the team of designers and programmers as a way to ensure that actual programming is likely to match design specifications. Catching errors at the pseudocode stage is less costly than catching them later in the development process. Once the pseudocode is accepted, it is rewritten using the vocabulary and syntax of a programming language. Pseudocode is sometimes used in conjunction with computer-aided software engineering-based methodologies.

It is possible to write programs that will convert a given pseudocode language into a given programming language.

1.6. Algorithm vs Pseudocode

An algorithm is a well-defined sequence of steps that provides a solution for a given problem, while a pseudocode is one of the methods that can be used to represent an algorithm. While algorithms can be written in natural language, pseudocode is written in a format that is closely related to high level programming language structures. But pseudocode does not use specific programming language syntax and therefore could be understood by programmers who are familiar with different programming languages. Additionally, transforming an algorithm presented in pseudocode to programming code could be much easier than converting an algorithm written in natural language.

1.7. How Does One become a Programmer?

A programmer is generally tasked with producing a solution to a problem via a computer program, which can be reused as various particular instances of that problem arise. To accomplish this task, the programmer therefore must be able to **understand the problem, derive an appropriate solution**, and then be able to **effectively express that solution**in a computer programming language.

The first prerequisite to becoming a programmer is to develop a strong background in problem solving as is often required in fields such as mathematics and engineering. The ability to formally, concisely, and clearly state a problem and then derive its solution is a fundamental skill that precedes the process of any computer coding. The study of computer algorithms focuses on the generalized problem solving approaches often applicable in computer science. Techniques such as programming design patterns provide practical templates which often help frame solutions in an understandable, reusable manner. In general, there are many different classes of problems in computer science that require different techniques to solve effectively: having a strong repertoire of approaches aids in finding good solutions.

The second prerequisite to becoming a programmer is knowing a programming language with which to express a particular solution to a problem. A programming language is a tool, which practice will help hone into expertise. Learning multiple languages can often be helpful as the process will demonstrate the particular strengths of different approaches to solving particular classes of problems.

In both these areas, practice is essential. Exposure to a wide variety of problems and tools to solve them will increase your understanding of the field as whole, to judge for yourself the relative merit of techniques in the field, as well as to discover unique, new approaches to addressing the problems of computer science. As with the practice of any new skill, do not be afraid to make mistakes, to redo earlier work, or to stumble along the way to expertise.

Don't be afraid to make mistakes because you *will* make them—constantly and for the rest of your career. Even the best programmers make mistakes regularly (if they try to say differently then they are either lying or deluded). Making mistakes is really part of the programing process. Someone said, to find a solution to a problem you must partly solve the problem. So you'll probably end up rewriting parts of your programs several times. Part of what distinguishes better programmers is their ability to catch at least some mistakes before they become a problem. Nobody can catch them all without help. Well, nobody can catch them all : there is no bug-free program. Additionally, it is good coding practice to code the smallest modules of a program, one at a time. This provides an isolated testing environment. Just be sure that everything is planned carefully from the outset, so that the little modules are not "orphaned" from other modules that they need to run. Note that when this approach is used, care should be taken to lay the foundation first, making careful note of "dependencies" within the program; code modules upon which other modules rely first, and then code higher-level modules after the foundations have been thoroughly tested. Unit testing is a good programming practice. Some programming processes, such as XP (eXtreme Programming), recommend to write tests *before* actual code.

Learn to work with others in a team environment. People have different strengths and weaknesses and a good team can bring together people whose strengths and weaknesses are complementary. The members of a team can teach each other. Most importantly, teams can tackle problems that would be too big for an individual. Beware, though, teams are **not** easy to lead and you can easily make a project a disaster by just gathering as many people as you can. If you want to work with a team, come with a solid design and a strong vision of what the project should look like when it's finished. If other members of the team suggest new ideas, take them with consideration but do not fall in the feature-greed pitfall, e.g. your project is never finished because the final goal grows beyond all proportions. As the XP process suggest, make small and frequent releases, prefer **running** code to vague and abstract design.

CHAPTER 2

WELCOME TO THE WORLD OF 'C'

2.1. Welcome to the World of C Programming

C is a general-purpose programming language which features economy of expression, modern control flow and data structures, and a rich set of operators. C is not a "very high level" language, nor a "big" one, and is not specialized to any particular area of application. But its absence of restrictions and its generality make it more convenient and effective for many tasks than supposedly more powerful languages.

The history of C programming language is quite interesting. C was originally designed for and implemented on the UNIX operating system on the DEC PDP-ll, by Dennis Ritchie.

In the 1960s Ritchie worked, with several other employees of Bell Labs (AT&T), on a project called Multics.

The goal of the project was to develop an operating system for a large computer that could be used by a thousand users. In 1969 AT&T (Bell Labs) withdrew from the project, because the project could not produce an economically useful system. So the employees of Bell Labs (AT&T) had to search for another project to work on (mainly Dennis M. Ritchie and Ken Thompson).

Ken Thompson began to work on the development of a new file system. He wrote, a version of the new file system for the DEC PDP-7, in assembler. (The new file system was also used for the game Space Travel).

Soon they began to make improvements and add expansions. (They used there knowledge from the Multics project to add improvements). After a while a complete system was born. Brian W. Kernighan called the system UNIX, a sarcastic reference to Multics. The whole system was still written in assembly code.

Besides assembler and Fortran, UNIX also had an interpreter for the programming language B. (The B language is derived directly from Martin Richards BCPL). The language B was developed in 1969-70 by Ken Thompson. In the early days computer code was written in assembly code.

To perform a specific task, you had to write many pages of code. A high-level language like B made it possible to write the same task in just a few lines of code. The language B was used for further development of the UNIX system. Because of the high-level of the B language, code could be produced much faster, then in assembly.

A drawback of the B language was that it did not know data-types. (Everything was expressed in machine words). Another functionality that the B language did not provide was the use of "structures".

The lag of these things formed the reason for Dennis M. Ritchie to develop the programming language C. So in 1971-73 Dennis M. Ritchie turned the B language into the C language, keeping most of the language B syntax while adding data-types and many other changes.

The C language had a powerful mix of high-level functionality and the detailed features required to program an operating system.

Therefore many of the UNIX components were eventually rewritten in C (the Unix kernel itself was rewritten in 1973 on a DEC PDP-11).

The programming language C was written down, by Kernighan and Ritchie, in a now classic book called "The C Programming Language, 1st edition". (Kernighan has said that he had no part in the design of the C language: "It's entirely Dennis Ritchie's work". But he is the author of the famous "Hello, World" program and many other UNIX programs).

2.2. Why Name "C" was Given to Language ?

1. Many of C's principles and ideas were derived from the earlier language B. (Ken Thompson was the developer of B Language.)
2. BCPL and CPL are the earlier ancestors of B Language
3. CPL is common Programming Language.In 1967, BCPL Language (Basic CPL) was created as a scaled down version of CPL
4. As many of the **features were derived from "B" Language thats why it was named as "C".**
5. After 7-8 years C++ came into existence which was first example of object oriented programming .

Feature of C Language

C Programming is widely used in Computer Technology, We can say that C is inspiration for development of other languages.

We can use C for different purposes. Below are some of the Features of C Programming –

2.3. Features of C Programming Language

Features of C	
Low Level Language Support	Program Portability
Powerful and Feature Rich	Bit Manipulation
High Level Features	Modular Programming
Efficient Use of Pointers	

1. *Low Level Features*

1. C Programming provides low level features that are generally provided by the Lower level languages. C is Closely Related to Lower level Language such as "**Assembly Language**".
2. It is easier to write assembly language codes in C programming.

2. *Portability*

1. C Programs are portable i.e they can be run on any Compiler with Little or no Modification.
2. Compiler and Preprocessor make it Possible for C Program to run it on Different PC.

3. *Powerful*

1. Provides Wide verity of '**Data Types**'.
2. Provides Wide verity of 'Functions'.
3. Provides useful Control & Loop Control Statements.

4. *Bit Manipulation*

1. C Programs can be manipulated using bits. We can perform different operations at bit level. We can manage memry representation at bit level. [Eg. We can use Structure to manage Memory at Bit Level].
2. It provides wide verity of bit manipulation Operators. We have bitwise operators to manage Data at bit level.

5. *High Level Features*

1. It is more User friendly as compare to Previous languages. Previous languages such as BCPL, Pascal and other programming languages never provide such great features to manage data.

2. Previous languages have there **pros and cons** but C Programming collected all useful features of previous languages thus C become **more effective language**.

6. *Modular Programming*

1. **Modular programming** is a software design technique that increases the extent to which software is composed of separate parts, called **modules.**
2. C Program Consist of Different Modules that are integrated together to form complete program.

7. *Efficient Use of Pointers*

1. Pointers has direct access to memory.
2. C Supports efficient use of pointer.

2.4. Application of C Programming

C Programming is best known programming language. C Programming is near to machine as well as human so it is called as Middle level Programming Language. C Programming can be used to do verity of tasks such as networking related,OS related.

Application of C Programming are Listed Below

1. C language is used for creating **computer applications.**
2. Used in writing **Embedded softwares.**
3. Firmware for various electronics, industrial and communications products which use micro-controllers.
4. It is also used in developing **verification software, test code, simulators**etc. for various applications and hardware products.
5. **For Creating Compiles** of different Languages which can take input from other language and convert it into lower level machine dependent language.
6. C is used to implement different **Operating System Operations**.
7. **UNIX kernel** is completely developed in C Language.

List of Applications of C Programming

List of Application		
Operating Systems	Network Drivers	Print Spoolers
Language Compilers	Assemblers	Text Editors
Modern Programs	Data Bases	Language Interpreters
Simulators	Utilities	Embedded System

2.5. Are you Ready to Write First Code in C?

Before starting the abcd of C language, you need to learn how to write, compile and run the first c program.

To write the first c program, open the C console and write the following code:

'Welcome to C' Example

AC program basically consists of the following parts.

- Preprocessor Commands.
- Functions.
- Variables.
- Statements & Expressions.
- Comments.

Let us look at a simple code that would print the words "Welcome to C" .

```
#include<stdio.h>
int main(){
/* my first program in C */
  printf("Welcome to the World of C Programming! \n");
return0;
}
```

Let us take a look at the various parts of the above program.

- The first line of the program *#include <stdio.h>* is a preprocessor command, which tells a C compiler to include stdio.h file before going to actual compilation.
- The next line *int main()* is the main function where the program execution begins.
- The next line /*...*/ will be ignored by the compiler and it has been put to add additional comments in the program. So such lines are called comments in the program.
- The next line *printf(...)* is another function available in C which causes the message "Hello, World!" to be displayed on the screen.

- The next line **return 0;** terminates the main() function and returns the value 0.

Compile and Execute C Program

Let us see how to save the source code in a file, and how to compile and run it. Following are the simple steps.

- Open a text editor and add the above-mentioned code.
- Save the file as *hello.c*
- Open a command prompt and go to the directory where you have saved the file.
- Type *gcc hello.c* and press enter to compile your code.
- If there are no errors in your code, the command prompt will take you to the next line and would generate *a.out* executable file.
- Now, type *a.out* to execute your program.
- You will see the output " Welcome to the World of C Programming! "printed on the screen.

```
$ gcc hello.c
$ ./a.out
Welcome to the World of C Programming!
```

Make sure the gcc compiler is in your path and that you are running it in the directory containing the source file hello.c.

Note: In this book all programs are executed in gcc compiler.

2.6. Execution Flow

Let's try to understand the flow of above program by the figure given below.

1. C program (source code) is sent to preprocessor first. The preprocessor is responsible to convert preprocessor directives into their respective values. The preprocessor generates an expanded source code.
2. Expanded source code is sent to compiler which compiles the code and converts it into assembly code.
3. The assembly code is sent to assembler which assembles the code and converts it into object code. Now a simple.obj file is generated.
4. The object code is sent to linker which links it to the library such as header files. Then it is converted into executable code. A simple.exe file is generated.

5. The executable code is sent to loader which loads it into memory and then it is executed. After execution, output is sent to console. Execution of c programming clearly mentioned in the following flow chart:

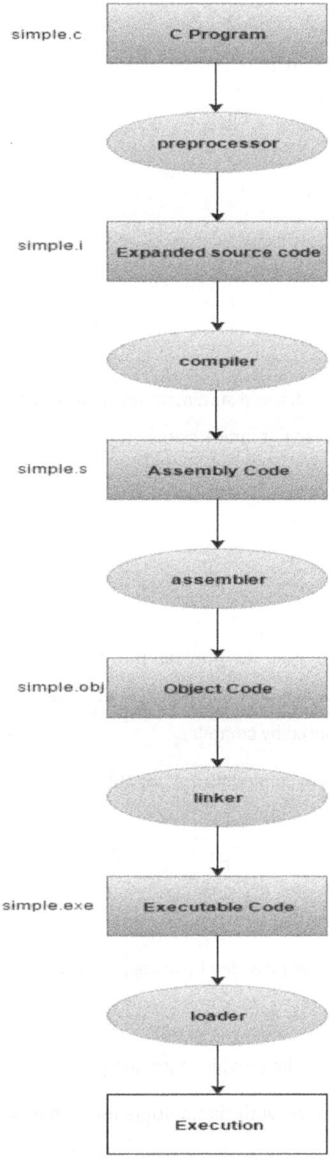

2.7. Tokens in C

A C program consists of various tokens and a token is either a keyword, an identifier, a constant, a string literal, or a symbol. For example, the following C statement consists of five tokens.

```
printf("Hello, World! \n");
```

The individual tokens are:

```
printf
(
"Hello, World! \n"
)
;
```

Semicolons

In a C program, the semicolon is a statement terminator. That is, each individual statement must be ended with a semicolon. It indicates the end of one logical entity. Given below are two different statements.

```
printf("Hello, World! \n");
return0;
```

Comments in C

Generally **Comments** are used to provide the description about the Logic written in program. Comments are not display on output screen. When we are used the comments, then that specific part will be ignored by compiler.

In 'C' language two types of comments are possible.

- Single line comments.
- Multiple line comments.

Single Line Comments

Single line comments can be provided by using / /....................

Multiple Line Comments

Multiple line comments can be provided by using /*......................*/

Note: When we are working with the multiple line comments then nested comments are not possible.

Rules for Writing Comments

1. **Program contains any number of comments at any place.**

Example

```
// header files
#include<stdio.h>
#include<conio.h>
void main()
{
// variable declaration
int a,b,c;
a=10;
b=20;
c=a+b;
printf("Sum= %d",c);
getch();
}
```

2. **Nested Comments are not possible, that means comments within comments.**

Example

```
void main()
{
/*
/*    comments  */
*/
}
```

3. **Comments can be splits over more than one line.**

Example

```
void main()
{
/* main
  function
  body part
*/
}
```

4. Comments are not case sensitive.

Example

```
void main()
{
/* MAIN Function BODY */
}
```

5. Single line comments start with "//"

Example

```
void main()
{
// Single line comment
}
```

Identifiers

A C identifier is a name used to identify a variable, function, or any other user-defined item. An identifier starts with a letter A to Z, a to z, or an underscore '_' followed by zero or more letters, underscores, and digits (0 to 9).

C does not allow punctuation characters such as @, $, and % within identifiers. C is a **case-sensitive** programming language. Thus, *Manpower*and *manpower* are two different identifiers in C. Here are some examples of acceptable identifiers.

```
MOHD    ZARA   ABC   MOVE_NAME  A_123
MYNAME50  _TEMP  J   A23B9   RETVAL
```

CHAPTER 3

C BASICS

3.1. Keywords in C

Keyword is a predefined or reserved word in C library with a fixed meaning and used to perform an internal operation. C Language supports 32 keywords.

Every **Keyword** exists in lower case latter like auto, break, case, const, continue, int etc.

32 Keywords in C Language

Auto	double	int	struct
Break	else	long	switch
Case	enum	register	typedef
Char	extern	return	union
Const	float	short	unsigned
Continue	for	signed	void
Default	goto	sizeof	volatile
Do	if	static	while

White Space in C

A line containing only whitespace, possibly with a comment, is known as a blank line, and a C compiler totally ignores it.

Whitespace is the term used in C to describe blanks, tabs, newline characters and comments. Whitespace separates one part of a statement from another and enables the compiler to identify where one element in a statement, such as int, ends and the next element begins. Therefore, in the following statement,

```
int age;
```

There must be at least one whitespace character (usually a space) between int and age for the compiler to be able to distinguish them. On the other hand, in the following statement.

```
fruit = apples + oranges;// get the total fruit
```

No whitespace characters are necessary between fruit and =, or between = and apples, although you are free to include some if you wish to increase readability.

3.2. C Variables

A variable is nothing but a name given to a storage area that our programs can manipulate. Each variable in C has a specific type, which determines the size and layout of the variable's memory; the range of values that can be stored within that memory; and the set of operations that can be applied to the variable.

The name of a variable can be composed of letters, digits, and the underscore character. It must begin with either a letter or an underscore. Upper and lowercase letters are distinct because C is case-sensitive. Based on the basic types explained in the previous chapter, there will be the following basic variable types.

Sr.No.	Type & Description
1	**Char** Typically a single octet(one byte). This is an integer type.
2	**Int** The most natural size of integer for the machine.
3	**Float** A single-precision floating point value.
4	**Double** A double-precision floating point value.
5	**Void** Represents the absence of type.

C programming language also allows to define various other types of variables, which we will cover in subsequent chapters like Enumeration, Pointer, Array, Structure, Union, etc. For this chapter, let us study only basic variable types.

Variable Definition in C

A variable definition tells the compiler where and how much storage to create for the variable. A variable definition specifies a data type and contains a list of one or more variables of that type as follows.

```
type variable_list;
```

Here, **type** must be a valid C data type including char, w_char, int, float, double, bool, or any user-defined object; and **variable_list** may consist of one or more identifier names separated by commas. Some valid declarations are shown here –

```
int i, j, k;

char c, ch;

float f, salary;

double d;
```

The line **int i, j, k;** declares and defines the variables i, j, and k; which instruct the compiler to create variables named i, j and k of type int.

Variables can be initialized (assigned an initial value) in their declaration. The initializer consists of an equal sign followed by a constant expression as follows –

type variable_name = value;

Some examples are:

```
extern int d = 3, f = 5;    // declaration of d and f.
int d = 3, f = 5;           // definition and initializing d and f.
byte z = 22;                // definition and initializes z.
char x = 'x';               // the variable x has the value 'x'.
```

For definition without an initializer: variables with static storage duration are implicitly initialized with NULL (all bytes have the value 0); the initial value of all other variables are undefined.

Variable Declaration in C

A variable declaration provides assurance to the compiler that there exists a variable with the given type and name so that the compiler can proceed for further compilation without requiring the complete detail about the variable. A variable definition has its meaning at the time of compilation only, the compiler needs actual variable definition at the time of linking the program.

A variable declaration is useful when you are using multiple files and you define your variable in one of the files which will be available at the time of linking of the program. You will use the keyword **extern** to declare a variable at any place. Though you can declare a variable multiple times in your C program, it can be defined only once in a file, a function, or a block of code.

Example

Try the following example, where variables have been declared at the top, but they have been defined and initialized inside the main function.

```
#include<stdio.h>
// Variable declaration:
externint a, b;
externint c;
externfloat f;
int main (){
```

```
/* variable definition: */
int a, b;
int c;
float f;
/* actual initialization */
  a =10;
  b =20;
  c = a + b;
  printf("value of c : %d \n", c);
  f =70.0/3.0;
  printf("value of f : %f \n", f);
return0;
}
```

When the above code is compiled and executed, it produces the following result.

```
value of c : 30
value of f : 23.333334
```

The same concept applies on function declaration where you provide a function name at the time of its declaration and its actual definition can be given anywhere else. For example.

```
// function declaration
int func();
int main(){
// function call
int i = func();
}
// function definition
int func(){
return0;
}
```

Lvalues and Rvalues in C

There are two kinds of expressions in C.

- **lvalue** – Expressions that refer to a memory location are called "lvalue" expressions. An lvalue may appear as either the left-hand or right-hand side of an assignment.
- **rvalue** – The term rvalue refers to a data value that is stored at some address in memory. An rvalue is an expression that cannot have a value assigned to it which means an rvalue may appear on the right-hand side but not on the left-hand side of an assignment.

Variables are lvalues and so they may appear on the left-hand side of an assignment. Numeric literals are rvalues and so they may not be assigned and cannot appear on the left-hand side. Take a look at the following valid and invalid statements.

```
int g = 20; // valid statement
10 = 20; // invalid statement; would generate compile-time error
```

3.3. Data Types in C

Data types in c refer to an extensive system used for declaring variables or functions of different types. The type of a variable determines how much space it occupies in storage and how the bit pattern stored is interpreted.

The types in C can be classified as follows.

Sr.No.	Types & Description
1	**Basic Types** They are arithmetic types and are further classified into: (a) integer types and (b) floating-point types.
2	**Enumerated types** They are again arithmetic types and they are used to define variables that can only assign certain discrete integer values throughout the program.
3	**The type void** The type specifier *void* indicates that no value is available.
4	**Derived types** They include (a) Pointer types, (b) Array types, (c) Structure types, (d) Union types and (e) Function types.

The array types and structure types are referred collectively as the aggregate types. The type of a function specifies the type of the function's return value.

We will see the basic types in the following section, where as other types will be covered in the upcoming chapters.

Integer Types

The following table provides the details of standard integer types with their storage sizes and value ranges.

Type	Storage size	Value range
char	1 byte	-128 to 127 or 0 to 255
unsigned char	1 byte	0 to 255
signed char	1 byte	-128 to 127
int	2 or 4 bytes	-32,768 to 32,767 or -2,147,483,648 to 2,147,483,647
unsigned int	2 or 4 bytes	0 to 65,535 or 0 to 4,294,967,295
short	2 bytes	-32,768 to 32,767
unsigned short	2 bytes	0 to 65,535
long	4 bytes	-2,147,483,648 to 2,147,483,647
unsigned long	4 bytes	0 to 4,294,967,295

To get the exact size of a type or a variable on a particular platform, you can use the **sizeof** operator. The expressions *sizeof(type)* yields the storage size of the object or type in bytes. Given below is an example to get the size of int type on any machine.

```
#include <stdio.h>
#include <limits.h>
int main() {
  printf("Storage size for int : %d \n", sizeof(int));
  return 0;
}
```

When you compile and execute the above program, it produces the following result on Linux.

```
Storage size for int : 4
```

Floating-Point Types

The following table provide the details of standard floating-point types with storage sizes and value ranges and their precision.

Type	Storage size	Value range	Precision
float	4 byte	1.2E-38 to 3.4E+38	6 decimal places
double	8 byte	2.3E-308 to 1.7E+308	15 decimal places
long double	10 byte	3.4E-4932 to 1.1E+4932	19 decimal places

The header file float.h defines macros that allow you to use these values and other details about the binary representation of real numbers in your programs.

The following example prints the storage space taken by a float type and its range values.

```
#include <stdio.h>
#include <float.h>
int main() {
  printf("Storage size for float : %d \n", sizeof(float));
  printf("Minimum float positive value: %E\n", FLT_MIN );
  printf("Maximum float positive value: %E\n", FLT_MAX );
  printf("Precision value: %d\n", FLT_DIG );
  return 0;
}
```

When you compile and execute the above program, it produces the following result on Linux.

```
Storage size for float : 4
Minimum float positive value: 1.175494E-38
Maximum float positive value: 3.402823E+38
Precision value: 6
```

The Void Type

The void type specifies that no value is available. It is used in three kinds of situations.

Sr.No.	Types & Description
1	**Function returns as void** There are various functions in C which do not return any value or you can say they return void. A function with no return value has the return type as void. For example, **void exit (int status);**
2	**Function arguments as void** There are various functions in C which do not accept any parameter. A function with no parameter can accept a void. For example, **int rand(void);**
3	**Pointers to void** A pointer of type void * represents the address of an object, but not its type. For example, a memory allocation function **void *malloc(size_t size);** returns a pointer to void which can be casted to any data type.

3.4. C Input and Output Operation

Input means to provide the program with some data to be used in the program and **Output** means to display data on screen or write the data to a printer or a file.

C programming language provides many built-in functions to read any given input and to display data on screen when there is a need to output the result.

All these built-in functions are present in C header files, we will also specify the name of header files in which a particular function is defined while discussing about it.

The C language is accompanied by a collection of library functions which includes a number of input/output functions. These functions are used to permit the transfer of information between the computer and the standard input/output device. The basic input/output functions are getchar, putchar, puts, scanf and printf. The first two functions, getchar and putchar, are used to transfer single characters. The next function puts is used to output strings, and the last two functions, scanf and printf, permit the transfer of single characters, numerical values and strings.

An input/output function can be accessed from anywhere within a program simply by writing the function name, followed by a list of arguments enclosed in parentheses. The arguments represent data items that are sent to the function. Some input/output functions do not require arguments, though the empty parentheses must still appear.

The names of those functions that return data items may appear within expressions, as though each function reference were an ordinary variable (eg, c=getchar();), or they may be referenced as separate statements (eg, scanf(...);). Some functions do not return any data items. Such functions are referenced as though they were separate statements (eg, putchar(...);).

C includes a collection of header files that provide necessary information in support of the various library functions. Each file generally contains information in support of a group of related library functions. These files are entered into the program via an #include statement at the beginning of the program. As a rule, the header file required by the standard input/output library functions is called stdio.h.

scanf() and printf() functions

The standard input-output header file, named stdio.h contains the definition of the functions printf() and scanf(), which are used to display output on screen and to take input from user respectively.

```
#include<stdio.h>
void main()
{
// defining a variable
  int i;
/*
```

```
        displaying message on the screen
        asking the user to input a value
    */
    printf("Please enter a value...");
    /*
        reading the value entered by the user
    */
    scanf("%d",&i);
    /*
        displaying the number as output
    */
    printf("\nYou entered: %d", i);
}
```

When you will compile the above code, it will ask you to enter a value. When you will enter the value, it will display the value you have entered on screen.

Single Character Input: the getchar Function

The getchar function is a part of the standard C input/output library. It returns a single character from a standard input device (typically a keyboard). The function does not require any arguments, though a pair of empty parentheses must follow the word getchar.

In general, a function reference would be written as:

character variable = getchar( );

where **character variable** refers to some previously declared character variable.

If an end-of-file condition is encountered when reading a character with the getchar function, the value of the symbolic constant EOF will automatically be returned. (This value will be assigned within the stdio.h file. Typically, the EOF will be assigned the value -1). The detection of EOF in this manner offers a convenient way to detect an end of file, whenever and wherever it may occur. Appropriate corrective action may then be taken.

The getchar function can also be used to read multi-character strings by reading one character at a time within a multi-pass loop.

Single Character Output: the Putchar Function

Single characters can be displayed using the C library function putchar. This function is complementary to the character input function getchar.

The putchar function like getchar is a part of the standard C input/output library. It transmits a single character to the standard output device (the computer screen). The character being transmitted will be represented as a character-type variable. It must be expressed as an argument to the function, enclosed in parentheses, following the word putchar.

In general, a function reference would be written as:

putchar(character variable)

where **character variable** refers to some previously declared character variable.

A simple example demonstrating the use of getchar and putchar is given below:

```
#include<stdio.h>
int main()
{
char c;
printf("n Please enter a character:");
c=getchar();
printf("n The character entered is: ");
putchar(c);
return 0;
}
```

In the above program, the statement c=getchar(); accepts a character entered by the user and stores it in the variable c. The character entered by the user can be anything from the C character set. The statement putchar(c); prints the character stored in the variable c.

The putchar function can be used to output a string constant by storing the string within a one-dimensional character-type array. Each character can then be written separately within a loop. The most convenient way to do this is to utilize the for statement, which we will discuss in future.

Entering Input Data: the scanf Function

Input data can be entered from a standard input device by means of the C library function scanf. This function can be used to enter any combination of numeric values, single characters and strings. The function returns the number of data items that have been entered successfully.

In general terms, the scanf function is written as:

scanf(control string, arg1, arg2,.........,argN)

Where **control string** refers to a string containing certain required formatting information, and **arg1,arg2,....,argN** are arguments that represent the individual data items. (Actually the arguments represent **pointers** that indicate the **addresses** of the data items within the computer's memory. We will discuss pointers in greater detail in a future article, but until then it would be helpful to remember the fact that the arguments in the scanf function actually represent the addresses of the data items being entered.)

The control string consists of the individual group of characters called **format specifiers**, with one character group for each input data item. Each character group must begin with a per cent sign (%) and be followed by a **conversion character** which indicates the type of the data item. Within the control string, multiple character groups can be contiguous, or they can be separated by whitespace characters (ie, white spaces, tabs or newline characters).

The most commonly used conversion characters are listed below:

Conversion Character	Data type of input data
c	character
d	decimal integer
e	floating point value
f	floating point value
g	floating point value
h	short integer
i	decimal, hexadecimal or octal integer
o	octal integer
x	hexadecimal integer
s	string
u	unsigned decimal integer
[. . .]	string which may include whitespace characters

The arguments to a scanf function are written as variables or arrays whose types match the corresponding character groups in the control string. Each variable name must be preceded by an **ampersand (&)**. However, character array names do not begin with an ampersand. The actual values of the arguments must correspond to the arguments in the scanf function in number, type and order. If two or more data items are entered, they must be separated by whitespace characters. The data items may continue onto two or more lines, since the newline character is considered to be a whitespace character and can therefore separate consecutive data items.

Example 1

```
#include<stdio.h>
int main()
{
char a[20];
int  i;
float b;
printf(" n Enter the value of a, i and b");
scanf("%s %d %f", a, &i, &b);
return 0;
}
```

In the above program, within the scanf function, the **control string** is "%s %d %f". It denotes three-character groups or format specifiers. The first format specifier %sdenotes that the first argument a represents a string (character array), the second format specifier %d denotes that the second argument i is an integer and the third format specifier %f denotes that the third argument b is a floating point number.

Also note that the only argument not preceded by an ampersand (&) is a since adenotes a character array.

The **s-type** conversion character applies to **a string that is terminated by a whitespace character**. Therefore a string that **includes whitespace characters** cannot be entered in this manner. To do so, there are two ways:

1. The s-type conversion character is replaced by a sequence of characters enclosed in square brackets, designated as [. . .]. Whitespace characters are also included in the string so that a string that contains whitespaces may be read.

When the program is executed, successive characters will continue to be read as long as each input character matches one of the characters enclosed in the square brackets. The order of the characters in the square brackets need not correspond to the order of the characters being entered. As soon as an input character is encountered that does not match one of the characters within the brackets, the scanffunction will stop reading any more characters and will terminate the string. A null character will then automatically be added to the end of the string.

Example

```
#include<stdio.h>
int main()
{
char line[80];
scanf(" %[ ABCDEFGHIJKLMNOPQRSTUVWXYZ]", line);
printf("%s", line);
return 0;
}
```

If the input data is:

READING A STRING WITH WHITE SPACES

Then the entire data will be assigned to the array line. However, if the input is:

Reading A String With white Spaces

Then only the letters in uppercase (R, A, S, W, S) will be assigned to line, as all the characters in the control string are in uppercase.

To enter a string that includes whitespaces as well as uppercase and lowercase characters we can use the **circumflex, ie (^)**, followed by a newline character within the brackets.

Example

```
scanf("[^n]", line);
```

The circumflex causes the subsequent characters within the square brackets to be interpreted in the opposite manner. Thus, when the program is executed, characters will be read as long as a newline character is not encountered.

Reading Numbers: Specifying Field Width

The consecutive non-whitespace characters that define a data item collectively define a **field**. To limit the number of such characters for a data item, an unsigned integer indicating the **field width** precedes the conversion character. The input data may contain fewer characters than the specified field width. Extra characters will be ignored.

Example: If a and b are two integer variables and the following statement is being used to read their values:

```
scanf( "%3d %3d", &a, &b);
```

and if the input data is: 1 4

then a will be assigned 1 and b 4.

If the input data is 123 456 then a=123 and b=456.

If the input is 1234567, then a=123 and b=456. 7 is ignored.

If the input is 123 4 56 (space inserted by a typing mistake), then a=123 and b=4. This is because the space acts as a data item separator.

Assignment Suppression

The **%** sign is followed by an asterisk **(*)** to skip over a data item without assigning it to the designated variable or array.

Example

```
scanf( "%s %*d %f", a, &i,&b);
```

If the input is: Alice 12 34.5 then a=Alice and b= 34.5. However, 12 will not be assigned to i because of the asterisk which is interpreted as an **assignment suppression character**.

Prefixes

Certain conversion characters within the control string can be preceded by a prefix; for example, an l or L to indicate a long integer argument and an h to indicate a short integer argument. Therefore "%ld" will indicate a long integer.

Difference between scanf() and gets()

The main difference between these two functions is that scanf() stops reading characters when it encounters a space, but gets() reads space as character too.

If you enter name as **Study Tonight** using scanf() it will only read and store **Study** and will leave the part after space. But gets() function will read it completely.

3.5. Memory Layout of C Programming

Before talking of memory layout of a C program and its various segments to store data and code instructions we should first understand that a compiler driver (that invokes the language preprocessor, compiler, assembler, and linker, as needed on behalf of the user) can generate three types of object files depending upon the options supplied to the compiler driver. Technically an object file is a sequence of bytes stored on disk in a file.

These object files are as follows:

- ***Relocatable object file:*** These are static library files. Static linkers such as the Unix ld program take collection of relocatable object files and command line arguments as input and generate a fully linked executable object file as output that can be loaded into memory and run. Relocatable object files contain binary code and data in a form that can be combined with other relocatable object files at compile time to create an executable object file.
- ***Executable object file:*** These are executable files contain binary code and data in a form that can be copied directly into memory and executed.
- ***Shared object file:*** These special type of relocatable object files are loaded into memory and linked dynamically, at either load time or run time.

Object files have a specific format, however this format may vary from system to system. Some most prevalent formats are .coff (Common Object File Format), .pe(Portable Executable), and elf (Executable and Linkable Format).

Code and Data Segments

However, the actual layout of a program's in-memory image is left entirely up to the operating system, and often the program itself as well. This article focus on the concepts of code and data segments of a program and does not take any specific platform into account. For a running program both the machine instructions (program code) and data are stored in the same memory space. The memory is logically divided into text and data segments. Modern systems use a single text segment to store program instructions, but more than one segment for data, depending upon the storage class of the data being stored there.

These segments can be described as follows:

1. Text or Code Segment.
2. Initialized Data Segments.
3. Uninitialized Data Segments.
4. Stack Segment.
5. Heap Segment.

Text or Code Segment

Code segment, also known as *text segment* contains machine code of the compiled program. The text segment of an executable object file is often read-only segment that prevents a program from being accidentally modified.

Data Segments

Data segment stores program data. This data could be in form of initialized or uninitialized variables, and it could be local or global. Data segment is further divided into four sub-data segments (initialized data segment, uninitialized or .bss data segment, stack, and heap) to store variables depending upon if they are local or global, and initialized or uninitialized.

Initialized Data or Data Segment

***Initialized data* or simply *data segment* stores** all global, static, constant, and external variables (declared with extern keyword) that are initialized beforehand.

Uninitialized Data or .bss Segment

Contrary to initialized data segment, ***uninitialized data*** or *.bss segment* stores all uninitialized global, static, and external variables (declared with extern keyword). Global, external, and static variable are by default initialized to zero. This section occupies no actual space in the object file; it is merely a place holder. Object file formats distinguish between initialized and uninitialized variables for space efficiency; uninitialized variables do not have to occupy any actual disk space in the object file.

Randal E. Bryant explains in his famous book on *Computer Systems: A Programmer's Perspective,* **Why is uninitialized data called .bss?** The use of the term .bss to denote uninitialized data is universal. It was originally an acronym for the "Block Storage Start" instruction from the IBM 704 assembly language (circa 1957) and the acronym has stuck. A simple way to remember the difference between the .data and .bss sections is to think of "bss" as an abbreviation for "Better Save Space!"

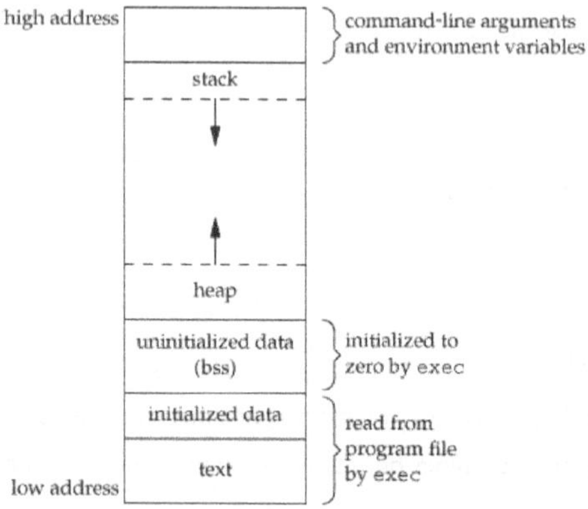

Stack Segment

The stack area traditionally adjoined the heap area and grew the opposite direction; when the stack pointer met the heap pointer, free memory was exhausted. (With modern large address spaces and virtual memory techniques they may be placed almost anywhere, but they still typically grow opposite directions.)

The stack area contains the program stack, a LIFO structure, typically located in the higher parts of memory. On the standard PC x86 computer architecture it grows toward address zero; on some other architectures it grows the opposite direction. A "stack pointer" register tracks the top of the stack; it is adjusted each time a value is "pushed" onto the stack. The set of values pushed for one function call is termed a "stack frame"; A stack frame consists at minimum of a return address.

Stack, where automatic variables are stored, along with information that is saved each time a function is called. Each time a function is called, the address of where to return to and certain information about the caller's environment, such as some of the machine registers, are saved on the stack. The newly called function then allocates room on the stack for its automatic and temporary variables. This is how recursive functions in C can work. Each time a recursive function calls itself, a new stack frame is used, so one set of variables doesn't interfere with the variables from another instance of the function.

Examples

The size(1) command reports the sizes (in bytes) of the text, data, and bss segments. (for more details please refer man page of size(1))

1. **Check the following simple C program**

```
#include <stdio.h>
int main(void)
{
  return 0;
}
```

Output (Only in gcc compiler)

```
text   data   bss   dec    hex  filename
960    248    8     1216   4c0  memory-layout
```

2. **Let us add one global variable in program, now check the size of bss (highlighted in red color).**

```
#include <stdio.h>
int global; /* Uninitialized variable stored in bss*/
int main(void)
{
  return 0;
}
```

Output (Only in gcc compiler)

```
text   data   bss   dec    hex  filename
960    248    12    1220   4c4  memory-layout
```

3. **Let us add one static variable which is also stored in bss.**

```
#include <stdio.h>
int global; /* Uninitialized variable stored in bss*/
int main(void)
{
  static int i; /* Uninitialized static variable stored in bss */
  return 0;
}
```

Output (Only in gcc compiler)

```
text   data   bss   dec    hex  filename
960    248    16    1224   4c8  memory-layout
```

4. **Let us initialize the static variable which will then be stored in Data Segment (DS)**

```
#include <stdio.h>
int global; /* Uninitialized variable stored in bss*/
int main(void)
{
  static int i = 100; /* Initialized static variable stored in DS*/
  return 0;
}
```

Output (Only in gcc compiler)

```
text   data   bss   dec    hex  filename
960    252    12    1224   4c8  memory-layout
```

5. Let us initialize the global variable which will then be stored in Data Segment (DS)

```
#include <stdio.h>
int global = 10; /* initialized global variable stored in DS*/
int main(void)
{
   static int i = 100; /* Initialized static variable stored in DS*/
   return 0;
}
```

Output (Only in gcc compiler)

```
text   data   bss   dec    hex  filename
960    256    8     1224   4c8  memory-layout
```

3.6. Operators in C

An operator is a symbol that tells the compiler to perform specific mathematical or logical functions. C language is rich in built-in operators and provides the following types of operators

- Arithmetic Operators.
- Relational Operators.
- Logical Operators.
- Bitwise Operators.
- Assignment Operators.
- Misc Operators.
- Increment and Decrement Operators.

Arithmetic Operators

The following table shows all the arithmetic operators supported by the C language. Assume variable **A** holds 10 and variable **B** holds 20 then –

Examples

Operator	Description	Example
+	Adds two operands.	A + B = 30
–	Subtracts second operand from the first.	A – B = -10
*	Multiplies both operands.	A * B = 200
/	Divides numerator by de-numerator.	B / A = 2
%	Modulus Operator and remainder of after an integer division.	B % A = 0
++	Increment operator increases the integer value by one.	A++ = 11
--	Decrement operator decreases the integer value by one.	A-- = 9

Relational Operators

The following table shows all the relational operators supported by C. Assume variable **A** holds 10 and variable **B** holds 20 then

Examples

Operator	Description	Example
==	Checks if the values of two operands are equal or not. If yes, then the condition becomes true.	(A == B) is not true.
!=	Checks if the values of two operands are equal or not. If the values are not equal, then the condition becomes true.	(A != B) is true.
>	Checks if the value of left operand is greater than the value of right operand. If yes, then the condition becomes true.	(A > B) is not true.
<	Checks if the value of left operand is less than the value of right operand. If yes, then the condition becomes true.	(A < B) is true.
>=	Checks if the value of left operand is greater than or equal to the value of right operand. If yes, then the condition becomes true.	(A >= B) is not true.
<=	Checks if the value of left operand is less than or equal to the value of right operand. If yes, then the condition becomes true.	(A <= B) is true.

Logical Operators

Following table shows all the logical operators supported by C language. Assume variable **A** holds 1 and variable **B** holds 0, then

Examples

<table>
<tr><th>Operator</th><th>Description</th><th>Example</th></tr>
<tr><td>&&</td><td>Called Logical AND operator. If both the operands are non-zero, then the condition becomes true.</td><td>(A && B) is false.</td></tr>
<tr><td>||</td><td>Called Logical OR Operator. If any of the two operands is non-zero, then the condition becomes true.</td><td>(A || B) is true.</td></tr>
<tr><td>!</td><td>Called Logical NOT Operator. It is used to reverse the logical state of its operand. If a condition is true, then Logical NOT operator will make it false.</td><td>!(A && B) is true.</td></tr>
</table>

Bitwise Operators

Bitwise operator works on bits and perform bit-by-bit operation. The truth tables for &, |, and ^ is as follows

<table>
<tr><th>P</th><th>Q</th><th>p & q</th><th>p | q</th><th>p ^ q</th></tr>
<tr><td>0</td><td>0</td><td>0</td><td>0</td><td>0</td></tr>
<tr><td>0</td><td>1</td><td>0</td><td>1</td><td>1</td></tr>
<tr><td>1</td><td>1</td><td>1</td><td>1</td><td>0</td></tr>
<tr><td>1</td><td>0</td><td>0</td><td>1</td><td>1</td></tr>
</table>

Assume A = 60 and B = 13 in binary format, they will be as follows –

A = 0011 1100

B = 0000 1101

A&B = 0000 1100

A|B = 0011 1101

A^B = 0011 0001

~A = 1100 0011

The following table lists the bitwise operators supported by C. Assume variable 'A' holds 60 and variable 'B' holds 13, then

Examples

Operator	Description	Example
&	Binary AND Operator copies a bit to the result if it exists in both operands.	(A & B) = 12, i.e., 0000 1100
|	Binary OR Operator copies a bit if it exists in either operand.	(A | B) = 61, i.e., 0011 1101
^	Binary XOR Operator copies the bit if it is set in one operand but not both.	(A ^ B) = 49, i.e., 0011 0001
~	Binary Ones Complement Operator is unary and has the effect of 'flipping' bits.	(~A) = -60, i.e,. 1100 0100 in 2's complement form.
<<	Binary Left Shift Operator. The left operands value is moved left by the number of bits specified by the right operand.	A << 2 = 240 i.e., 1111 0000
>>	Binary Right Shift Operator. The left operands value is moved right by the number of bits specified by the right operand.	A >> 2 = 15 i.e., 0000 1111

Assignment Operators

The following table lists the assignment operators supported by the C language.

Examples

Operator	Description	Example
=	Simple assignment operator. Assigns values from right side operands to left side operand	C = A + B will assign the value of A + B to C
+=	Add AND assignment operator. It adds the right operand to the left operand and assign the result to the left operand.	C += A is equivalent to C = C + A
-=	Subtract AND assignment operator. It subtracts the right operand from the left operand and assigns the result to the left operand.	C -= A is equivalent to C = C - A
*=	Multiply AND assignment operator. It multiplies the right operand with the left operand and assigns the result to the left operand.	C *= A is equivalent to C = C * A
/=	Divide AND assignment operator. It divides the left operand with the right operand and assigns the result to the left operand.	C /= A is equivalent to C = C / A
%=	Modulus AND assignment operator. It takes modulus using two operands and assigns the result to the left operand.	C %= A is equivalent to C = C % A
<<=	Left shift AND assignment operator.	C <<= 2 is same as C = C << 2
>>=	Right shift AND assignment operator.	C >>= 2 is same as C = C >> 2
&=	Bitwise AND assignment operator.	C &= 2 is same as C = C & 2
^=	Bitwise exclusive OR and assignment operator.	C ^= 2 is same as C = C ^ 2
|=	Bitwise inclusive OR and assignment operator.	C |= 2 is same as C = C | 2

Misc Operators ↦ Size of & Ternary

Besides the operators discussed above, there are a few other important operators including **sizeof** and **? :** supported by the C Language.

Examples

Operator	Description	Example
sizeof()	Returns the size of a variable.	sizeof(a), where a is integer, will return 4.
&	Returns the address of a variable.	&a; returns the actual address of the variable.
*	Pointer to a variable.	*a;
? :	Conditional Expression.	If Condition is true ? then value X : otherwise value Y

Increment and Decrement Operator

C programming allows the use of **++** and **–** operators which are increment and decrement operators respectively. Both the increment and decrement operators are unary operators. The increment operator ++ adds 1 to the operand and the decrement operator – subtracts 1 from the operand. The general syntax of these operators are:

Increment Operator: *m++ or ++m;*

Decrement Operator: *m--or --m;*

In the example above, *m++* simply means *m=m+1;* and *m--* simply means *m=m-1;*

Increment and decrement operators are mostly used in for and while loops.

++m and *m++* performs the same operation when they form statements independently but they function differently when they are used in right hand side of an expression.

++m is known as prefix operator and *m++* is known as postfix operator. A prefix operator firstly adds 1 to the operand and then the result is assigned to the variable on the left whereas a postfix operator firstly assigns value to the variable on the left and then increases the operand by 1. Same is in the case of decrement operator.

For example,

X=10;

Y=++X;

In this case, the value of X and Y will be 6.

And,

X=10;

Y=X++;

In this case, the value of Y will be 10 and the value of X will be 11.

3.7. Operators Precedence in C

Operator precedence determines the grouping of terms in an expression and decides how an expression is evaluated. Certain operators have higher precedence than others; for example, the multiplication operator has a higher precedence than the addition operator.

For example, x = 7 + 3 * 2; here, x is assigned 13, not 20 because operator * has a higher precedence than +, so it first gets multiplied with 3*2 and then adds into 7. Here, operators with the highest precedence appear at the top of the table, those with the lowest appear at the bottom. Within an expression, higher precedence operators will be evaluated first.

Examples

OPERATOR	DESCRIPTION	ASSOCIATIVITY
()	Parentheses (function call)	left-to-right
[]	Brackets (array subscript)	
.	Member selection via object name	
->	Member selection via pointer	
++/-	Postfix increment/decrement	
++/-	Prefix increment/decrement	right-to-left
+/-	Unary plus/minus	
!~	Logical negation/bitwise complement	
(type)	Cast (convert value to temporary value of type)	
*	Dereference	
&	Address (of operand)	
sizeof	Determine size in bytes on this implementation	
*,/,%	Multiplication/division/modulus	left-to-right
+/-	Addition/subtraction	left-to-right
<>	Bitwise shift left, Bitwise shift right	left-to-right
< , <=	Relational less than/less than or equal to	left-to-right
> , >=	Relational greater than/greater than or equal to	left-to-right
== , !=	Relational is equal to/is not equal to	left-to-right
&	Bitwise AND	left-to-right
^	Bitwise exclusive OR	left-to-right
|	Bitwise inclusive OR	left-to-right
&&	Logical AND	left-to-right
||	Logical OR	left-to-right
?:	Ternary conditional	right-to-left
=	Assignment	right-to-left
+= , -=	Addition/subtraction assignment	
*= , /=	Multiplication/division assignment	
%= , &=	Modulus/bitwise AND assignment	
^= , |=	Bitwise exclusive/inclusive OR assignment	
<>=	Bitwise shift left/right assignment	
,	expression separator	left-to-right

3.8. Exercises

1) What will be the output of the C program?

```
#include<stdio.h>
int main()
{
        char num = '\010';
        printf("%d", num);
        return 0;
}
```

A. 010

B. 08

C. 10

D. 8

Answer: Option: D

Explanation

The value of a variable num is '\010'. Which means the character with value 10 in octal, which is 8 in decimal.

2) What will be the output of the C program?

```
#include<stdio.h>
int main()
{
        void num=10;
        printf("%v", num);
        return 0;
}
```

A. Compilation error

B. 10

C. Garbage value

D. 0

Answer: Option: A

Explanation

Void is not a valid data type for declaring variables.

3) What will be the output of the C program?

```
#include<stdio.h>
int main()
{
        void *ptr;
        int num = 10;
        ptr = &num;
        printf("%d", ptr);
        return 0;
}
```

A. 10

B. Compilation error

C. 0

D. Address

Answer: Option: D

Explanation

Though, void is not a valid data type for declaring variables. It is a valid for declaring pointer variable *ptr thus printf displays the address of a normal variable num

4) What will be the output of the C program?

```
#include<stdio.h>
int main()
{
        printf("%d\t",sizeof(2.5));
        printf("%d\t",sizeof(2));
        printf("%d",sizeof('A'));
        return 0;
}
```

A. 8 4 2

B. 8 4 1

C. 4 4 1

D. 2.5 2 A

Answer: Option: B

Explanation

C compiler by default will assign any undeclared float data type as double. Thus 841 is outputted.

5) What will be the output of the C program?

```
#include<stdio.h>
int main(){
        signed a;
        unsigned b;
        a = 6u + -16 + 16u + -6;
        b = a + 1;
        if(a == b)
        printf("%d %d",a,b);
        else
        printf("%u %u",a, b);
        return 0;
}
```

A. Compilation error

B. 0 0

C. 0 1

D. address address

Answer: Option: C

Explanation

Clearly, a != b and it execute the else part, where we ask compiler to display the value of a and b.

6) Which of the following data type is right C programming?

```
#include<stdio.h>
int main(){
        int num = - -2;
        printf("num = %d", num);
        return 0;
}
```

A. Runtime error

B. Compilation error

C. -2

D. 2

Answer: Option: D

Explanation

Minus and minus are get multiplied, thus the result is 2.

7) What will be the output of the C program?

```
#include<stdio.h>
int main()
{
        float a = 5.0;
        printf ("Result is = %d ", (24 / 5) * a);
        return 0;
}
```

A. 20.000000

B. 20

C. Runtime error

D. 0

Answer: Option: D

Explanation

Output must be 20.000000. As we use %d as a format specifier, it displays 0

8) What will be the output of the C program?

```
#include<stdio.h>
int main()
{
        10;
        printf("%d", 10);
}
```

A. Compilation Error

B. 10

C. Runtime error

D. No output

Answer: Option: B

Explanation

10; is an executable statement. So it doesn't end up with compilation error.

9) What will be the output of the C program neglecting user input?

```
#include<stdio.h>
int main()
{
        enum fruits{ apple, mango } ;
        printf("%d %d", apple, mango);
        return 0;
}
```

A. Compilation error

B. 1 2

C. 0 1

D. Runtime error

Answer: Option: C

Explanation

The values of apple, mango are available in fruits by default enum keyword initialize its value from 0 to n.

10) What will be the output of the C program?

```
#include<stdio.h>
int main()
{
        printf(" %%% ");
        return 0;
}
```

A. %

B. No output

C. %%

D. %%%

Answer: Option: A

Explanation

Alternative % are treated as format specifier and it won't display.

11) What will be the output of the C program?

```
#include<stdio.h>
int main()
{
        int num = 8;
        printf ("%d %d", num << 1, num >> 1);
        return 0;
}
```

A. 7 9

B. 4 16

C. 9 7

D. 16 4

Answer: Option: D

Explanation

Shift operator shift the value stored in a variable num. One to the right(<<) and other to the left(>>).

12) What will be the output of the C program?

```
#include<stdio.h>
int main()
{
        int i = 5;
        int a = ++i + ++i;
        printf("%d",a);
        return 0;
}
```

A. 14

B. 13

C. 12

D. 11

Answer: Option: A

Explanation

How 14 comes instead of 13. Let's explain it.

Actually a = 6 + 7;, but not because second (++) operators result will be overwritten to the first operand.

Note that even if you have n number of operands with increment operator(++). the above discussed effect will take place only between first and second operand

13) What will be the output of the C program?

```
#include<stdio.h>
int main()
{
        int i = 5;
        int a = ++i + ++i + ++i;
        printf("%d",a);
        return 0;
}
```

A. 24

B. 23

C. 21

D. 22

Answer: Option: D

Explanation

Now we go straight way to the program.

a = ++i + ++i + ++i;

a = 6 + ++i + ++i

a = 6 + 7 + ++i

a = 7 + 7 + ++i

a = 7 + 7 + 8

a = 7 + 7 + 8

Finally a = 22.

14) What will be the output of the C program?

```
#include<stdio.h>
int main(){
        int i = 16;
        i =! i > 15;
        printf("i = %d",i);
        return 0;
}
```

A. 16

B. 1

C. 0

D. Compilation error

Answer

Option: C

Explanation

Note !i which means for any value of variable i to 0.

Now, we have the condition i = 0 > 14;. Thus i = 0 (condition false) will is outputted.

15) What will be the output of the C program?

```
#include<stdio.h>
int main()
{
        int i = 5;
        int a = --i - --i - --i - --i;
        printf("%d",a);
        return 0;
}
```

A. -2

B. -3

C. -1

D. -4

Answer: Option: D

Explanation

Now we go straight way to the program.

a = --i - --i - --i - --i;

a = 4 - --i - --i - --i

a = 4 - 3 - --i - --i

a = 3 - 3 - --i - --i

a = 3 - 3 - 2 - --i

a = 3 - 3 - 2 - 1

Finally a = -3.

16) What will be the output of the C program?

```
#include<stdio.h>

int main()

{

        int a = 2, b = 2, c = 0, d = 2, m;

        m = a++ && b++ && c++ || d++;

        printf("%d %d %d %d %d",a, b, c, d, m);

        return 0;

}
```

A. Compilation error

B. 3 3 1 3 1

C. 3 3 1 3 0

D. some garbage value

Answer: Option: B

Explanation

As operator enjoys priority && have more priority than ||.

m = a++ && b++ && c++ || d++;

m = 1 && c++ || d++;

m = 1 || d++;

m = 1 || 0;

m = 1;

17) What will be the output of the C program?

```
#include<stdio.h>
int main()
{
        int a = 5;
        a = 1, 2, 3;
        printf("%d", a);
        return 0;
}
```

A. 3

B. 5

C. compilation error

D. 1

Answer: Option: D

Explanation

Priority for the values assigned to any variable is given from left to right.

18) What will be the output of the C program?

```
#include<stdio.h>

int main()

{

        int a;

        a = (1, 2, 3);
```

```
        printf("%d", a);
        return 0;
}
```

A. 8

B. 9

C. 7

D. 6

Answer: Option: A

Explanation

Priority for the values inside a brackets () assigned to any variable is given from right to left.

19) What will be the output of the C program?

```
#include<stdio.h>
int main()
{
        int x[10] = {0, 1, 2, 3, 4, 5, 6, 7, 8, 9};
        printf("%d",sizeof(x));
        return 0;
}
```

A. 2

B. 4

C. 20

D. 40

Answer: Option: D

Explanation

Now we go straight way to the program. Here x is an array variable which holds 10 integer values. Thus sizeof int is 4, then 4 * 10 =40.

20) What will be the output of the C program?

```
#include<stdio.h>
int main()
{
```

```
        unsigned int num = -4;
        printf("%d", ~num);
        return 0;
}
```

A. Compilation error

B. 3

C. 4

D. some garbage value

Option: B

Explanation

~ is a One's Complement bitwise operator.

The function of ~ is a One's Complement is to inverse all value only after converting a decimal value to binary 0's and 1's

Here int num = -4;

which is num = -100 (in binary 0's and 1's)

~num = +011 (in binary 0's and 1's)

~num = 3

21) What will be the output of the C program?

```
#include<stdio.h>
int main()
{
        int x = 2;
        (x & 1) ? printf("true") : printf("false");
        return 0;
}
```

A. Compilation error

B. true

C. false

D. Runtime error

Answer: Option: C

Explanation

As & is a unary operator we have to assume all decimal values to binary(0's and 1's)

int x = 2 (in decimal)

x = 00000010(in decimal 0's and 1's)

Now we go for condition (00000010 & 00000001)

Clearly, condition false as it leads to 0 when multiplied.

Try By Yourself

1) What will be the output of the C program?

```
#include<stdio.h>
int main()
{
        int a = 4, b = 2;
        printf("a^b = %d", a^b);
        return 0;
}
```

A. 12

B. 10

C. 8

D. 6

2) What will be the output of the C program?

```
#include<stdio.h>

int main()

{

        int a = 4, b = 2;

        printf("a|b = %d\n", a|b);

        return 0;

}
```

A. 6

B. 7

C. 5

D. 4

3) What will be the output of the C program?

```
#include<stdio.h>
int main()
{
		int a = 7, b = 4, c = 2;
		printf("a|b&c = %d\n", a|b&c);
		return 0;
}
```

A. 3

B. 8

C. 6

D. 7

4) What will be the output of the C program?

```
#include<stdio.h>

int main()

{

		int a = 7, b = 4, c = 2;

		printf("a|b&c = %d\n", a|b&c);

		return 0;

}
```

A. 3

B. 8

C. 6

D. 7

5) What will be the output of the C program?

```
#include<stdio.h>
int main()
{
		int s[3] = {'\0', '\0'};
		int x[3] = {'\0', '\0'};
		int c = s[1] + x[0];
		printf("%d",c);
		return 0;
}
```

A. Compilation error

B. 0

C. No Output

D. some garbage value

6) What will be the output of the C program?

```
#include<stdio.h>

int main()

{

        int a = NULL - true;

        printf("%d",a);

        return 0;

}
```

A. Compilation error

B. 1

C. -1

D. Runtime error

7) What will be the output of the C program?

```
#include<stdio.h>

int main()

{

        printf("%d",3 * 2--);

}
```

A. 3

B. 9

C. 6

D. Compilation error

8) What will be the output of the C program?

```
#include<stdio.h>

int main()

{

        int a = 1, b = 3, c;
```

```
        c = b << a;
        b = c * (b * (++a)--);
        a = a >> b;
        printf("%d",b);
        return 0;
}
```

A. 36

B. Compilation error

C. 30

D. 24

9) What will be the output of the C program?

```
#include<stdio.h>
int main()
{
        int i = 10;
        i++;
        i * i;
        printf("%d\n",i);
        return 0;
}
```

A. 121

B. 100

C. 10

D. 11

10) What will be the output of the C program?

```
#include<stdio.h>
        #define x =
int main()
{
        int a;
```

```
        a x 5;
        printf("%d",a);
        return 0;
}
```

A. Compilation error

B. Runtime error

C. 5

D. program incomplete

Answer

1)d 2)a 3)d 4)b 5)c 6)d 7)a 8)d 9)c 10)c

CHAPTER 4

CONTROL STATEMENTS

4.1. Introduction

Statements

Statements are the instructions given to the computer to perform any kind of action. Action may be in the form of data movement, decision making etc. Statements form the smallest executable unit within a C program. Statements are always terminated by semicolon.

Compound Statement

A compound statement is a grouping of statements in which each individual statement ends with a semi-colon. The group of statements is called block. Compound statements are enclosed between the pair of braces ({ }). The opening brace ({) signifies the beginning and closing brace (}) signifies the end of the block.

Null Statement

Writing only a semicolon indicates a null statement. Thus ';' is a null or empty statement. This is quite useful when the syntax of the language needs to specify a statement but the logic of the program does not need any statement. This statement is generally used in for and while looping statements.

Control statements enable us to specify the flow of program control; ie, the order in which the instructions in a program must be executed. They make it possible to make decisions, to perform tasks repeatedly or to jump from one section of code to another. The statements that are used to control the flow of execution of statements are known as conditional control statements.

Conditional statements are divided into three types:

1. Conditional.
2. Unconditional.
3. Looping.

Conditional Control Statements

A 'c 'program is a set of statements which are normally executed sequentially in the order in which they appear. This happens when no options (or) no repetitions of certain calculations are necessary. However in practice we have a number of situations where we may have to change the order of execution of statements until certain specified conditions are met. This involves a kind of "decision making" to see whether a particular condition has occurred (or0 not & then direct the computer to execute certain statements accordingly.

'C' language passes such decision making capabilities & supports the following statements known as conditional (or) decision making statements.

1. if statements.
2. switch statement.
3. conditional operator statement.

4.2. If Statements

The 'if' statement is a powerful decision making statement and is used to control the flow of execution of statements. It is basically a two way decision statement and is used in conjunction with as expression. It takes the following form:-

if(test expression)

It allows the computer to evaluate the expression first & then depending on whether the value of the expression (relation(or)condition) is 'true'(non-zero)or 'false'(zero),it transfer the control to a particular statement. This point of program has two paths follow, one for true condition & the other for the false condition.

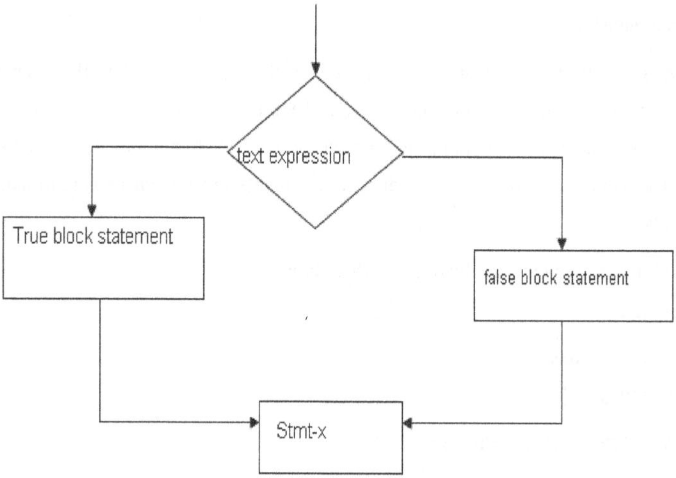

The if statement may be implemented in different forms depending on the complexity of condition to be tested.

1. simple if statement.
2. if ...else statement.
3. nested if ...else statement.
4. else if ladder.

Simple If Statements

This is the most simple form of the branching statements.

It takes an expression in parenthesis and an statement or block of statements. if the expression is true then the statement or block of statements gets executed otherwise these statements are skipped.

Syntax

```
if (test expression)
{
  statement 1;
  .................
  statement n;
}
statement x;
```

Flowchart of If Statement

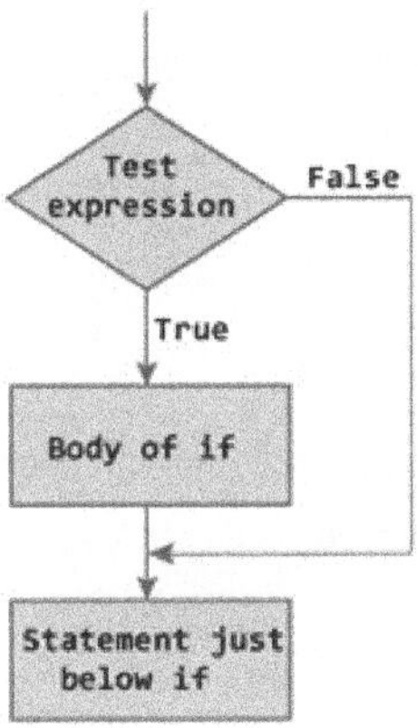

Flow of if Statement

The if statement evaluates the test expression inside the parenthesis.

If the test expression is evaluated to true (nonzero), statements inside the body of if is executed.

If the test expression is evaluated to false (0), statements inside the body of if is skipped from execution.

Example #1: C If Statement

```
// Program to display a number if user enters negative number
// If user enters positive number, that number won't be displayed
#include<stdio.h>
int main()
{
int number;
  printf("Enter an integer: ");
  scanf("%d",&number);
// Test expression is true if number is less than 0
if(number <0)
{
    printf("You entered %d.\n", number);
}
  printf("The if statement is easy.");
return0;
}
```

Output 1

```
Enter an integer: -2
You entered -2.
The if statement is easy.
```

When user enters -2, the test expression (number < 0) becomes true. Hence, You entered -2is displayed on the screen.

Output 2

Enter an integer: 5

The if statement in C programming is easy.

When user enters 5, the test expression (number < 0) becomes false and the statement inside the body of if is skipped.

4.3. If Else Statements

The if...else statement executes some code if the test expression is true (nonzero) and some other code if the test expression is false (0).

Syntax of If...Else

```
if (testExpression) {
  // codes inside the body of if
}
else {
  // codes inside the body of else
}
```

If test expression is true, codes inside the body of if statement is executed and, codes inside the body of else statement is skipped.

If test expression is false, codes inside the body of else statement is executed and, codes inside the body of if statement is skipped.

Flowchart of If...Else Statement

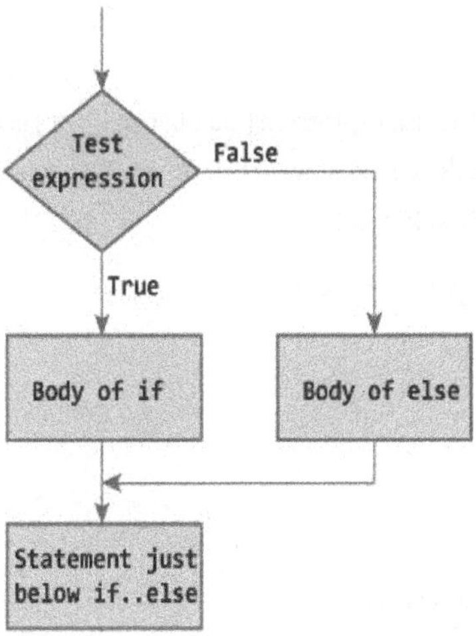

Flowchart of if... Else Statement

Example #1: C if...Else Statement

```
// Program to check whether an integer entered by the user is odd or even
#include<stdio.h>
int main()
{
int number;
  printf("Enter an integer: ");
  scanf("%d",&number);
// True if remainder is 0
if( number%2==0)
    printf("%d is an even integer.",number);
else
    printf("%d is an odd integer.",number);
return0;
}
```

Output

```
Enter an integer: 7
7 is an odd integer.
```

When user enters 7, the test expression (number%2 == 0) is evaluated to false. Hence, the statement inside the body of else statement printf("%d is an odd integer"); is executed and the statement inside the body of if is skipped.

Example#2: Program for leap year

```
#include <stdio.h>
void main()
{
   int yr;
   clrscr();
   printf("Enter a year:");
   scanf("%d", &yr);
   if ((yr%4 == 0) && ((yr%100 !=0) || (yr%400==0)))
     printf("It's a leap year...!!!!");
```

```
    else
        printf ("It's not a leap year....!!!");
}
```

Output

Enter a year: 1997

It's not a leap year...!!!

4.4. Nested if...else statement (if...elseif....else Statement)

The if...else statement executes two different codes depending upon whether the test expression is true or false. Sometimes, a choice has to be made from more than 2 possibilities.

The nested if...else statement allows you to check for multiple test expressions and execute different codes for more than two conditions.

Block Diagram for Nested If

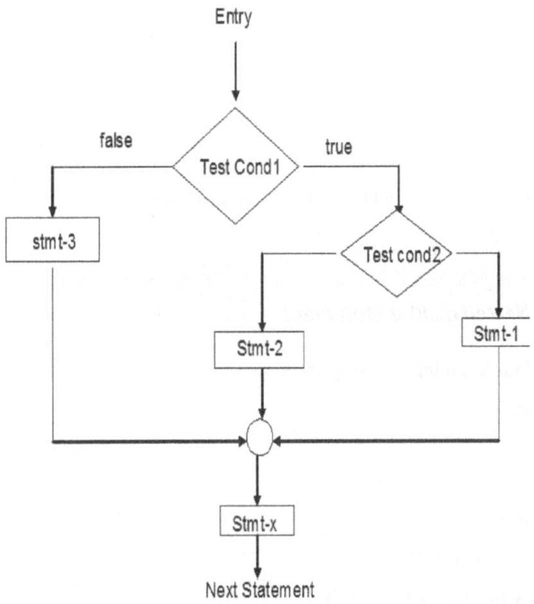

If the condition 1 is false , the statement-3 will be executed otherwise it continues to perform the second test . IF the condition-2 is true, the statement-1 is evaluated; otherwise statement -2 will be evaluated & then the control is transferred to statement-x.

Syntax of Nested If...Else Statement

```
if (testExpression1)
{
  // statements to be executed if testExpression1 is true
}
else if(testExpression2)
{
  // statements to be executed if testExpression1 is false and testExpression2 is true
}
else if (testExpression 3)
{
  // statements to be executed if testExpression1 and testExpression2 is false and
testExpression3 is true
}
.
.
else
{
  // statements to be executed if all test expressions are false
}
```

Example #1: C Nested If...Else Statement

```
// Program to relate two integers using =, > or <
#include<stdio.h>
int main()
{
int number1, number2;
  printf("Enter two integers: ");
  scanf("%d %d",&number1,&number2);
//checks if two integers are equal.
if(number1 == number2)
{
    printf("Result: %d = %d",number1,number2);
```

```
}
//checks if number1 is greater than number2.
elseif(number1 > number2)
{
    printf("Result: %d > %d", number1, number2);
}
// if both test expression is false
else
{
    printf("Result: %d < %d",number1, number2);
}
return0;
}
```

Output

```
Enter two integers: 12
23
Result: 12 < 23
```

4.5. The Else If Ladder

The if else ladder statement in C programming language is used to test set of conditions in sequence. An if condition is tested only when all previous if conditions in if-else ladder is false. If any of the conditional expression evaluates to true, then it will execute the corresponding code block and exits whole if-else ladder.

Syntax

```
if(expression 1)
{
  statement-block1;
}
elseif(expression 2)
{
  statement-block2;
```

```
}
elseif(expression 3)
{
  statement-block3;
}
else
  default-statement;
```

The expression is tested from the top (of the ladder) to downwards. As soon as the **true** condition will found, the statement associated with it is executed.

Else If Ladder Block Diagram

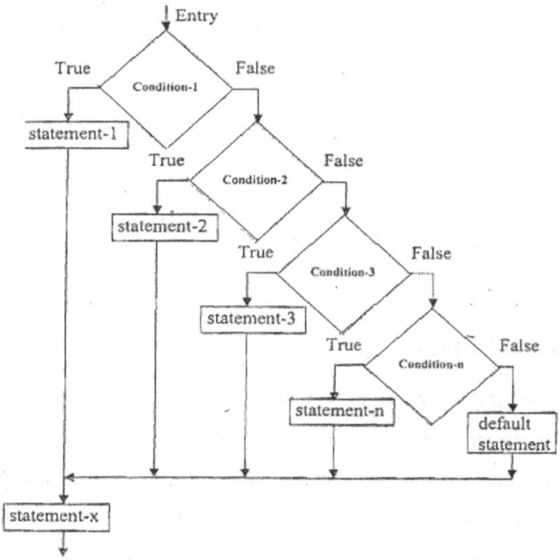

- First of all condition_expression_One is tested and if it is true then statement1 will be executed and control comes out out of whole if else ladder.
- If condition_expression_One is false then only condition_expression_Two is tested. Control will keep on flowing downward, If none of the conditional expression is true.
- The last else is the default block of code which will gets executed if none of the conditional expression is true.

Example

```
#include<stdio.h>
#include<conio.h>
int main(){
  int marks;
    printf("Enter your marks between 0-100\n");
  scanf("%d", &marks);
  /* Using if else ladder statement to print
    Grade of a Student */
  if(marks >= 90){
    /* Marks between 90-100 */
    printf("YOUR GRADE : A\n");
  } else if (marks >= 70 && marks < 90){
    /* Marks between 70-89 */
    printf("YOUR GRADE : B\n");
  } else if (marks >= 50 && marks < 70){
    /* Marks between 50-69 */
    printf("YOUR GRADE : C\n");
  } else {
    /* Marks less than 50 */
    printf("YOUR GRADE : Failed\n");
  }
      getch();
  return(0);
}
```

Above program check whether a student passed or failed in examination using if statement.

Output

```
Enter your marks
96
YOUR GRADE : A
Enter your marks
75
YOUR GRADE : B
Enter your marks
```

```
60
YOUR GRADE : C
Enter your marks
35
YOUR GRADE : Failed
```

4.6. Switch Case Statement

When you want to solve multiple option type problems, for example: Menu like program, where one value is associated with each option and you need to choose only one at a time, then, switch statement is used. Switch statement is a control statement that allows us to choose only one choice among the many given choices. The expression in switch evaluates to return an integral value, which is then compared to the values present in different cases. It executes that block of code which matches the case value. If there is no match, then **default** block is executed (if present). The general form of switch statement is

```
switch(expression)
{
  case value-1:
  block-1;
  break;
  case value-2:
  block-2;
  break;
  case value-3:
  block-3;
  break;
  case value-4:
  block-4;
    break;
  default:
    default-block;
  break;
}
```

The following rules apply to a **switch** statement.

- The **expression** used in a **switch** statement must have an integral or enumerated type, or be of a class type in which the class has a single conversion function to an integral or enumerated type.
- You can have any number of case statements within a switch. Each case is followed by the value to be compared to and a colon.
- The **constant-expression** for a case must be the same data type as the variable in the switch, and it must be a constant or a literal.
- When the variable being switched on is equal to a case, the statements following that case will execute until a **break** statement is reached.
- When a **break** statement is reached, the switch terminates, and the flow of control jumps to the next line following the switch statement.
- Not every case needs to contain a **break**. If no **break** appears, the flow of control will *fall through* to subsequent cases until a break is reached.
- A **switch** statement can have an optional **default** case, which must appear at the end of the switch. The default case can be used for performing a task when none of the cases is true. No **break** is needed in the default case.

Flow Diagram

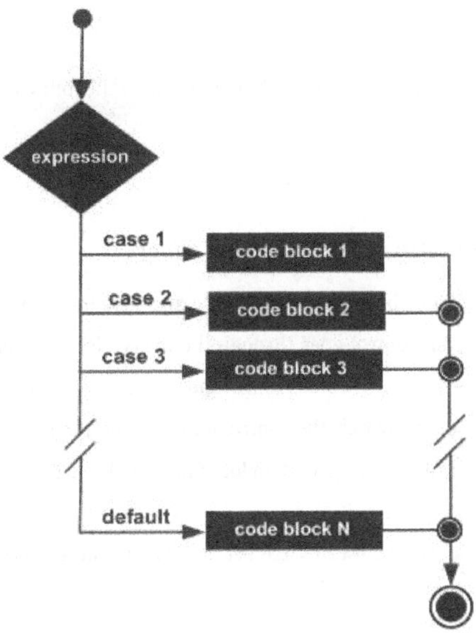

Example

```
#include <stdio.h>
int main () {
  /* local variable definition */
  char grade = 'B';
  switch(grade) {
    case 'A' :
      printf("Excellent!\n" );
      break;
    case 'B' :
    case 'C' :
      printf("Well done\n" );
      break;
    case 'D' :
      printf("You passed\n" );
      break;
    case 'F' :
      printf("Better try again\n" );
      break;
    default :
      printf("Invalid grade\n" );
  }
  printf("Your grade is  %c\n", grade );
  return 0;
}
```

When the above code is compiled and executed, it produces the following result –

```
Well done
Your grade is B
```

Difference between Switch Case and Else If Ladder

Here are the main **difference between switch case and else if ladder**

1. In *else if ladder*, the control goes through the every else if statement until it finds true value of the statement or it comes to the end of the else if ladder. In case of *switch case*, as per the value of the switch, the control jumps to the corresponding case.
2. The switch case is more compact than lot of nested else if. So, switch is considered to be more readable.
3. The use of break statement in switch is essential but there is no need of use of break in else if ladder.

4. The variable data type that can be used in expression of switch is integer only where as in else if ladder accepts integer type as well as character.
5. Another **difference between switch case and else if ladder** is that the *switch* statement is considered to be less flexible than the else if ladder, because it allows only testing of a single expression against a list of discrete values.
6. Since the compiler is capable of optimizing the switch statement, they are generally considered to be more efficient. Each case in switch statement is independent of the previous one. In case of else if ladder, the code needs to be processed in the order determined by the programmer.
7. *Switch case statement* work on the basis of equality operator whereas *else if ladder* works on the basis of true false (zero/non-zero) basis.

4.7. Exercises: (Use GCC Compiler)

1) What will be the output of the program?

```
#include<stdio.h>

int main()

{

  int a = 500, b = 100, c;

  if(!a >= 400)

    b = 300;

  c = 200;

  printf("b = %d c = %d\n", b, c);

  return 0;

}
```

A. b = 300 c = 200

B. b = 100 c = garbage

C. b = 300 c = garbage

D. b = 100 c = 200

Answer

Option D

Explanation

Initially variables a = 500, b = 100 and c is not assigned.

Step 1: if(!a >= 400)

Step 2: if(!500 >= 400)

Step 3: if(0 >= 400)

Step 4: if(FALSE) Hence the if condition is failed.

Step 5: So, variable c is assigned to a value '200'.

Step 6: printf("b = %d c = %d\n", b, c); It prints value of b and c.

Hence the output is "b = 100 c = 200"

2) What will be the output of the program?

```
#include<stdio.h>
int main()
{
int x = 3;
float y = 3.0;
if(x == y)
    printf("x and y are equal");
else
    printf("x and y are not equal");
return0;
}
```

A. x and y are equal

B. x and y are not equal

C. Unpredictable

D. No output

Answer

Option A

Explanation

Step 1: int x = 3; here variable x is an integer type and initialized to '3'.

Step 2: float y = 3.0; here variable y is an float type and initialized to '3.0'

Step 3: if(x == y) here we are comparing if(3 == 3.0) hence this condition is satisfied. Hence it prints "x and y are equal".

3) What will be the output of the program?

```
#include<stdio.h>
int main()
{
char ch;
if(ch = printf(""))
    printf("It matters\n");
else
    printf("It doesn't matters\n");
return0;
}
```

A. It matters

B. It doesn't matters

C. Matters

D. No output

Answer: Option **B**

Explanation

printf() returns the number of charecters printed on the console.

Step 1: if(ch = printf("")) here printf() does not print anything, so it returns '0'(zero).

Step 2: if(ch = 0) here variable ch has the value '0'(zero).

Step 3: if(0) Hence the if condition is not satisfied. So it prints the else statements.

Hence the output is "It doesn't matters".

Note: Compiler shows a warning "possibly incorrect assinment".

4) What will be the output of the program?

```
#include<stdio.h>
int main()
{
float a = 0.7;
if(0.7> a)
    printf("Hi\n");
else
    printf("Hello\n");
```

```
return0;
    }
```

A. Hi

B. Hello

C. Hi Hello

D. None of above

Answer

Option A

Explanation

if(0.7 > a) here a is a float variable and 0.7 is a double constant. The double constant 0.7 is greater than the float variable a.

Hence the if condition is satisfied and it prints 'Hi'

5) What will be the output of the program?

```
#include<stdio.h>
int main()
{
int a = 300, b, c;
if(a >= 400)
  b = 300;
  c = 200;
  printf("%d, %d, %d\n", a, b, c);
return0;
}
```

A. 300, 300, 200

B. Garbage, 300, 200

C. 300, Garbage, 200

D. 300, 300, Garbage

Answer

Option C

Explanation

Step 1: int a = 300, b, c; here variable a is initialized to '300', variable b and c are declared, but not initialized.

Step 2: if(a >= 400) means if(300 >= 400). Hence this condition will be failed.

Step 3: c = 200; here variable c is initialized to '200'.

Step 4: printf("%d, %d, %d\n", a, b, c); It prints "300, garbage value, 200". because variable b is not initialized.

6) What will be the output of the program?

```
#include<stdio.h>
int main()
{
int x = 10, y = 20;
if(!(!x) && x)
    printf("x = %d\n", x);
else
    printf("y = %d\n", y);
return0;
}
```

A. y =20

B. x = 0

C. x = 10

D. x = 1

Answer

Option C

Explanation

The logical not operator takes expression and evaluates to true if the expression is false and evaluates to false if the expression is true. In other words it reverses the value of the expression.

Step 1: if(!(!x) && x).

Step 2: if(!(!10) && 10).

Step 3: if(!(0) && 10).

Step 3: if(1 && 10).

Step 4: if(TRUE) here the if condition is satisfied. Hence it prints x = 10.

7) What is the output of this C code?

```
1. #include <stdio.h>
2. void main()
3. {
4. int x =0;
5. if(x =0)
6. printf("Its zero\n");
7. else
8. printf("Its not zero\n");
9. }
```

a) Its not zero

b) Its zero

c) Run time error

d) None

View Answer

Answer

a

Explanation

In Line Number 5 we have used assignment operator (=) instead of equal (==) operator

8) main()

```
{
int y;
scanf("%d",&y); // input given is 2000
if( (y%4==0 && y%100 != 0) || y%100 == 0 )
   printf("%d is a leap year");
else
   printf("%d is not a leap year");
}
```

Answer

2000 is a leap year

Explanation

An ordinary program to check if leap year or not.

9) The output of the code below is

```
#include <stdio.h>
void main()
{
   int x = 0;
   if (x == 0)
      printf("hi");
   else
      printf("how are u");
      printf("hello");
}
```

A) hi

B) how are you

C) hihello

D) Hello

Answer

C

Explanation

Compiler use to execute after the first statement of the else block.

10) What will be output if you will compile and execute the following c code?

```
void main(){
  int i=10;
  static int x=i;
  if(x==i)
    printf("Equal");
  else if(x>i)
    printf("Greater than");
  else
    printf("Less than");
}
```

(a) Equal

(b) Greater than

(c) Less than

(d) Compiler error

(e) None of above

Answer

(d)

Explanation

static variables are load time entity while auto variables are run time entity. We can not initialize any load time variable by the run time variable. In this example i is run time variable while x is load time variable.

11) What will be output if you will compile and execute the following c code?

```
void main(){
  if(printf("cquestionbank"))
    printf("I know c");
  else
    printf("I know c++");
}
```

(a) I know c

(b) I know c++

(c) cquestionbankI know c

(d) cquestionbankI know c++

(e) Compiler error

Answer

(c)

Explanation

Return type of printf function is integer which returns number of character it prints including blank spaces. So printf function inside if condition will return 13. In if condition any non- zero number means true so else part will not execute.

12) What will be the output of following program ?

```
#include <stdio.h>
intmain()
{
  inta=10;
  if(a==10)
  {
    printf("Hello...");
```

```
        break;
        printf("Ok");
    }
    else
    {
        printf("Hii");
    }
    return0;
}
```

A) Hello...

B) Hello...OK

C) OK

D) Error

Answer

D

Explanation

Error: misplaced break/ illegal break.

A break statement can be used with looping and switch statements.

13) What will be the output of following program?

```
#include <stdio.h>
intmain()
{
    if( (-100 && 100)||(20 && -20) )
        printf("%s","Condition is true.");
    else
        printf("%s","Condition is false.");
    return0;
}
```

A) Condition is true.

B) Condition is false.

C) No output

D) ERROR

Answer

A

Explanation

Condition is true.

Any non zero value is treated as true for conidion.

Consider the expressions: if((-100 && 100)||(20 && -20))

=if((1) || (1))

=if(1)

14) What will be the output of following program?

```
#include <stdio.h>

#define TRUE 1

intmain()

{

  if(TRUE)

     printf("1");

     printf("2");

  else

     printf("3");

     printf("4");

  return0;

}
```

A) ERROR

B) 1

C) 12

D) 2

Answer

A

Explanation

Misplaced if/illegal else without matching if. You can use only one statement within the if () without parenthesis {...}

15) What will be the output of following program?

```
#include <stdio.h>
intmain()
{
  intpn=100;
  if(pn>20)
    if(pn<20)
      printf("Heyyyyy");
  else
    printf("Hiiiii");
  return0;
}
```

A) No output

B) Hiiiii

C) Heyyyyy

D) HeyyyyyHiiiii

Answer

B

Explanations

Printf ("Hiiiii"); that is written after else, is treated as else part of inner if condition if (pn<20).

16) What will be output when you will execute following c code?

```
#include<stdio.h>
void main(){
   int check=2;
   switch(check){
     case 1: printf("D.W.Steyn");
     case 2: printf(" M.G.Johnson");
     case 3: printf(" Mohammad Asif");
     default: printf(" M.Muralidaran");
   }
}
```

A). M.G.Johnson

B). M.Muralidaran

C). M.G.Johnson Mohammad Asif M.Muralidaran

D.) Compilation error

E.) None of the above

Answer

Option C

Explanation

If we will not use break keyword in each case the program control will come in each case after the case witch satisfy the switch condition.

17) What will be the output of the C program?

```
#include<stdio.h>
int main()
{
        short int si = 1;
        switch(++si - si++)
        {
                case 1L:
                printf("First");
                break;
                case 2L:
                printf("Second");
                break;
                default:
                printf("Bye");
                break;
        }
return 0;
}
```

A. First

B. Bye

C. Second

D. Compilation Error

Answer

Option: B

Explanation

The switch (++si - si++) which becomes switch(2 - 2) -> switch(0) so default block gets executed.

18) What will be the output of the C program?

```
#include<stdio.h>
int main()
{
int i = 1;
for(i = 0; i<10; i+3)
        switch(i)
        {

                case 3:
                printf("Hai. This is case 3");
                break;
                case 6:
                printf("Hai. This is case 6");
                break;
                break;
                default:
                printf("Hai. This is default");
                break;

        }

return 0;
}
```

A. Hai. This is case 3

B. Hai. This is case 6

C. Infinite Execution

D. Hai. This is default

Answer

Option: C

Explanation

The for loop don't have a proper incrementation control. We don't have any other control to stop, so it goes infinite. There is extra break statement but it is unreachable code.

19) What will be the output of the C program?

```
#include<stdio.h>
int main(){
char ch = '\0';
switch(ch)
{
        case NULL:
        printf("Empty \0");
        break;
        case ' ':
        printf("Empty Empty");
        break;
        case '0':
        printf("Empty 0");
        break;
        default:
        printf("Nothing");
}
return 0;
}
```

A. Empty \0

B. Empty Empty

C. Empty 0

D. Empty

Answer

Option: D

Explanation

NULL = '\0'. So it executes case NULL: block. The printf statement should be like this printf("Empty \\0"); to print Empty \0.

20) What will be the output of the C program?

```
#include<stdio.h>
int main()
{
switch(25)
{
        case 25L:
        printf("25L");
        break;
        case 25.0:
        printf("25.0");
        break;
        default:
        printf("Nothing");
        break;
}
return 0;
}
```

A. 25L

B. 25.0

C. Compilation Error

D. Nothing

Answer

Option: C

Explanation

Compiler Error: Constant expression required

21) What will be the output of the C program?

```
#include<stdio.h>

int main(){

int num = 0;

if (num++, num--, ++num)

        switch(num)

        {

                case 1:

                printf("case one");

                break;

                case 2:

                printf("case two");

                break;

                default:

                printf("default block");

                break;

        }

  return 0;

}
```

A.case one

B.case two

C.default block

D.Compile Time Error

Answer

Option: A

Explanation

The if block gets executed because the expression will returns 1 and the value of num is 1 so case 1: block gets executed.

Try by Yourself

1) What is the output of this code?

```
#include <stdio.h>
int main()
{
   int x = 1;
   if (x > 0)
      printf("inside if\n");
   else if (x > 0)
      printf("inside elseif\n");
}
```

a) inside if

b) inside elseif

c) inside if

inside elseif

d) Compile time error

2) What is the output of this code?

```
#include <stdio.h>
int main()
{
   int x = 0;
   if (x++)
      printf("true\n");
   else if (x == 1)
      printf("false\n");
}
```

a) true

b) false

c) Compile time error

d) Undefined behavior

3) What is the output of this code?

```
#include <stdio.h>
int main()
{
```

```
    int x = 0;
    if (x == 1)
        if (x == 0)
            printf("inside if\n");
        else
            printf("inside else if\n");
    else
        printf("inside else\n");
}
```

a) inside if

b) inside else if

c) inside else

d) Compile time error

4) What is the output of this code?

```
#include <stdio.h>
int main()
{
    int x = 0;
    if (x == 0)
        printf("true, ");
    else if (x = 10)
        printf("false, ");
    printf("%d\n", x);
}
```

a) false, 0

b) true, 0

c) true, 10

d) Compile time error

5) What is the output of this code?

```
#include <stdio.h>
int main()
{
    int a = 1;
    if (a--)
```

```
        printf("True");
        if (a++)
            printf("False");
    }
```

a) True

b) False

c) True False

d) No Output

6) Comment on the output of this C code?

```
#include <stdio.h>
int main()
{
int a =1;
if(a)
printf("All is Well ");
printf("I am Well\n");
else
printf("I am not a River\n");
}
```

a)Output will be All is Well I am Well

b) Output will be I am Well I am not a River

c) Output will be I am Well

d) Compile time errors during compilation

7) if (a == 1||b == 2){} can be written as:

A) if (a == 1) if (b == 2){}

B) if (a == 1){} if (b == 2){}

C) if (a == 1){} else if (b == 2){}

D) None of the mentioned

8) What will be output if you will compile and execute the following c code?

```
void main(){
  int i=0;
  if(i==0){
    i=((5,(i=3)),i=1);
    printf("%d",i);
```

```
  }
  else
    printf("equal");
}
```

(a) 5

(b) 3

(c) 1

(d) equal

(e) None of above

9) What will be the output of following program?

```
#include <stdio.h>
voidmain()
{
  if(!printf(""))
    printf("Okkk");
  else
    printf("Hiii");
}
```

A) Okkk

B) Hiii

C) Error

D) None

10) What will be the output of following program?

```
#include <stdio.h>
void main()
{
  char val=1;
  if(val--==0)
    printf("TRUE");
  else
    printf("FALSE");
}
```

A)TRUE

B)FALSE

C)Error

D)None

11) What will be the output of the C program?

```
#include<stdio.h>
int main(){
int num = 5;
switch(num++ == 5)
{
        case 1:
        printf("TRUE");
        break;
        case 0:
        printf("FALSE");
        break;
        default:
        printf("inside default");
}
  return 0;
}
```

A. inside default

B. FALSE

C. TRUE

D. Compilation Error

12) What will be the output of the C program?

```
#include<stdio.h>
int main(){
char ch = 96.0;
switch(ch)
{
        case 96:
  printf("inside case");
        break;
  default:
```

```
    printf("inside default");
}
return 0;
}
```

A. inside case

B. inside default

C. Prints Nothing

D. Compilation Error

13) What will be the output of the C program?

```
#include<stdio.h>
int main(){
int i = 3, j = 4;
switch(i | j)
{
        case 1:
        printf("inside case 1");
        break;
        case 3:
        printf("inside case 3");
        break;
        case 4:
        printf("inside case 4");
        break;
        case 7:
        printf("inside case 7");
        break;
}
return 0;
}
```

A. inside case 1

B. inside case 3

C. inside case 4

D. inside case 7

14) What will be the output of the C program?

```
#include<stdio.h>
int main()
{
 int i = 0;
 while(i < 2)
 switch(i)
 {
          i = 2;
          case 0:
          printf("Hai. This is case 0");
  i++;
          case 1:
          printf("Hai. This is case 1");
  i++;
          break;
          case 2:
          printf("Hai. This is case 2");
  i++;
          break;
  default:
          printf("Hai. This is default");
  i++;
          break;
 }
 return 0;
}
```

A. Hai. This is case 0 Hai. This is case 1

B. Hai. This is case 0 Hai. This is case 2

C. Hai. This is case 0 Hai. This is case 1 Hai. This is case 2

D. Hai. This is case 0 Hai. This is default

15) What will be the output of the C program?

```
#include<stdio.h>
int main(){
int n = 4;
switch(n)
{
default:
printf("Hai default ");
case 1:
printf("Hai case 1 ");
case 2:
printf("Hai case 2 ");
case 3:
printf("Hai case 3 ");
}
return 0;
}
```

A. Runtime Error

B. Hai default

C. Compilation Error

D. Hai default Hai case 1 Hai case 2 Hai case 3

Answer

1)a 2)b 3)c 4)b 5)a 6)d 7)d 8)c 9)a 10)a 11)c 12)a 13)d 14)a 15)d

CHAPTER 5

LOOPING STATEMENTS

5.1. Introduction

You may encounter situations, when a block of code needs to be executed several number of times.

In general, statements are executed sequentially: The first statement in a function is executed first, followed by the second, and so on.

Programming languages provide various control structures that allow for more complicated execution paths. A loop statement allows us to execute a statement or group of statements multiple times.

5.2. Why Use Loop?

When you need to execute a block of code several number of times then you need to use looping concept in C language.

Advantage with looping statement.

- Reduce length of Code.
- Take less memory space.
- Burden on the developer is reducing.
- Time consuming process to execute the program is reduced.

Difference between Conditional and Looping Statement

Conditional statement executes only once in the program where as looping statements executes repeatedly several number of time.

Types of Loop Control Statements in C

There are 3 types of loop control statements in C language. They are,

1. For.
2. while.
3. do-while.

5.3. For Loop

A **For** loop is a repetition control structure that allows you to efficiently write a loop that needs to execute a specific number of times. The syntax of for loop is:

```
for (initializationStatement; testExpression; updateStatement)
{
    // codes
}
```

Here is the flow of control in a 'for' loop.

- The **init** step is executed first, and only once. This step allows you to declare and initialize any loop control variables. You are not required to put a statement here, as long as a semicolon appears.
- Next, the **condition** is evaluated. If it is true, the body of the loop is executed. If it is false, the body of the loop does not execute and the flow of control jumps to the next statement just after the 'for' loop.
- After the body of the 'for' loop executes, the flow of control jumps back up to the **increment** statement. This statement allows you to update any loop control variables. This statement can be left blank, as long as a semicolon appears after the condition.
- The condition is now evaluated again. If it is true, the loop executes and the process repeats itself (body of loop, then increment step, and then again condition). After the condition becomes false, the 'for' loop terminates.

Flow Diagram

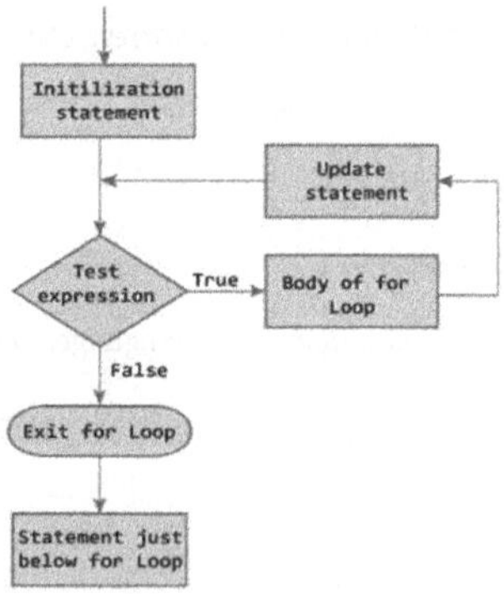

Flowchart of for Loop

The for loop is executed as follows:

1. It first evaluates the initialization code.
2. Then it checks the condition expression.
3. If it is **true**, it executes the for-loop body.
4. Then it evaluate the increment/decrement condition and again follows from step 2.
5. When the condition expression becomes **false**, it exits the loop

Example

```
// Program to calculate the sum of first n natural numbers

// Positive integers 1,2,3...n are known as natural numbers

#include <stdio.h>

int main()

{

  int num, count, sum = 0;

  printf("Enter a positive integer: ");

  scanf("%d", &num);

  // for loop terminates when n is less than count

  for(count = 1; count <= num; ++count)

  {

    sum += count;

  }

  printf("Sum = %d", sum);

  return 0;

}
```

Output

```
Enter a positive integer: 5

Sum = 15
```

Nested for loop

A for loop inside another for loop is called nested for loop.

Syntax of Nested for loop

```
for (initialization; condition; increment/decrement)
{
  statement(s);
  for (initialization; condition; increment/decrement)
  {
    statement(s);
    ... ... ...
  }
  ... ... ...
}
```

Flowchart of Nested for Loop

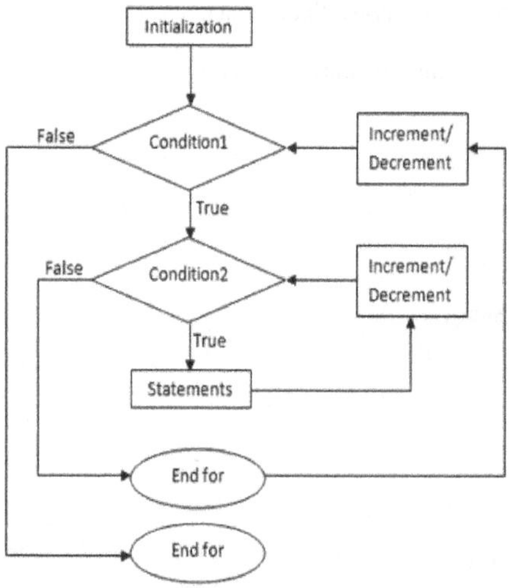

Flowchart for Nested For Loop

Example: C program to print all the composite numbers from 2 to a certain number entered by user.

```
#include<stdio.h>
#include<math.h>
int main()
{
  int i,j,n;
  printf("Enter a number:");
  scanf("%d",&n);
  for(i=2;i<=n;i++)
  {
    for(j=2;j<=(int)pow(i,0.5);j++)
    {
      if(i%j==0)
      {
        printf("%d is composite\n",i);
        break;
      }
    }
  }
  return 0;
}
```

Output

```
Enter a number: 15
4 is composite
6 is composite
8 is composite
9 is composite
10 is composite
12 is composite
14 is composite
15 is composite
```

A number is said to be composite if it has at least one factor other than 1 and itself. This program prints all the composite numbers starting from 2 to a certain number *n*, entered by user. We need to use a nested loop to solve this problem. The outer for loop runs from 2 to *n* and the inner loop is used to determine whether a number is composite or not. We need to check for that factor starting from 2 to integer part of square root of that number.

Consider 15, its square root is nearly 3.873. Here, the integer part is 3. Now, if there is a factor of 15 from 2 to 3 then it is composite. Here, 3 is a factor of 15. Hence, 15 is a composite number.

Infinite for Loop

An infinite loop (sometimes called an *endless loop*) is a piece of coding that lacks a functional exit so that it repeats indefinitely. In computer programming, a loop is a sequence of instruction s that is continually repeated until a certain condition is reached.

Typically, a certain process is done, such as getting an item of data and changing it, and then some condition is checked, such as whether a counter has reached a prescribed number. If the presence of the specified condition cannot be ascertained, the next instruction in the sequence tells the program to return to the first instruction and repeat the sequence, which typically goes on until the program terminates automatically after a certain duration of time, or the operating system terminates the program with an error.

A Common Way to Make an Endless Loop

```
#include <stdio.h>
int main()
{
 int x;
 for(x=0;x=10;x=x+1)
 {
 printf("What are you lookin' at?");
 }
 return(0);
}
```

The problem with the code in A Common Way to Make an Endless Loop is that the for statement's exit condition is always true: x=10

5.4. While Loop

The most basic loop in C is the while loop and it is used is to repeat a block of code. A while loop has one control expression (a specific condition) and executes as long as the given expression is true. Here is the syntax:

Syntax

```
while (condition)
{
statement(s);
}
```

In while loop first the condition (boolean expression) is tested; if it is false the loop is finished without executing the statement(s).

If the condition is true, then the statements are executed and the loop executes again and again until the condition is false. If there is only one statement, the braces may be omitted; however, it is good practice to always include the braces.

Flowchart of While Loop

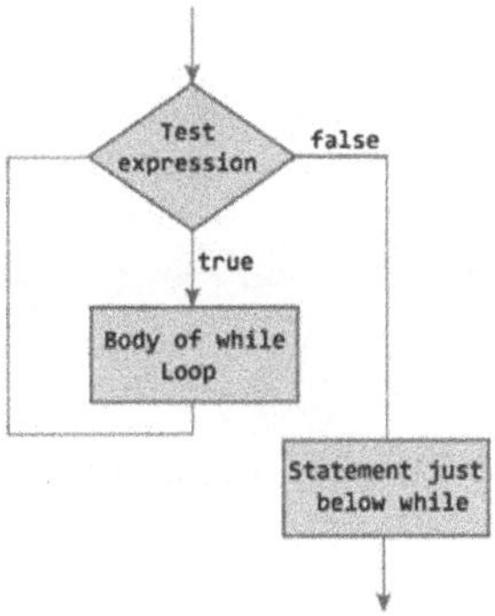

Flowchart of While Loop

How While Loop Works?

The while loop evaluates the test expression.

If the test expression is true (nonzero), codes inside the body of while loop are executed. The test expression is evaluated again. The process goes on until the test expression is false.

When the test expression is false, the while loop is terminated.

The following program prints n asterisks.

```
#include<stdio.h>
main()
{
   int x,ctr;
   x=0;
   printf("Input number of rows :");
   scanf("%d",&ctr);
   while(x<ctr)
     {
     printf("*");
     x++;
     }
}
```

suppose ctr = 5

	x	output
is x<ctr ?	0	*
is x<ctr ?	1	**
is x<ctr ?	2	***
is x<ctr ?	3	****
is x<ctr ?	4	*****
is x<ctr ?	5	exit from loop

Example

```
// Program to find factorial of a number
// For a positive integer n, factorial = 1*2*3...n
#include<stdio.h>
int main()
{
int number;
longlong factorial;
  printf("Enter an integer: ");
  scanf("%d",&number);
  factorial =1;
// loop terminates when number is less than or equal to 0
while(number >0)
{
factorial *= number;// factorial = factorial*number;
--number;
}
  printf("Factorial= %lld", factorial);
return0;
}
```

Output

```
Enter an integer: 5
Factorial = 120
```

Infinite While Loop

If the condition to be tested is always true, the loop will run forever i.e. infinite times. Such conditions should be avoided in programming. **For example,**

```
while (1)
{
  printf("This is infinite loop");
}
```

This loop will run infinitely. Here, we have kept a non zero value in place of condition so C compiler will treat it as true. To avoid such situation, we shouldn't use any non zero or non null value in place of condition.

To stop an infinite loop, break statement can be used. **For example,**

```
while (1)
{
  printf("This loop will run only once");
  break;
}
```

5.5. Difference between For and While Loop

The FOR loop is often used when you usually know how many times you would like the program, which means it will run that program until the number of times is complete before it terminates itself. The WHILE loop works in a similar manner but requires a conditional statement. Benefit of the WHILE loop is when you are unsure how many iterations are required to complete the given expression.

Loops are often in programming and are useful if one needs to execute a program multiple times. These are often great when dealing with repetitive programming. These are often confusing for people who are just learning how to program.

While both FOR and WHILE loop are used for similar purpose of dealing with repetitive program until the conditions required are satisfied, they are used in different situations. Let's understand each loop separately.

The FOR loop is often used when you usually know how many times you would like the program, which means it will run that program until the number of times is complete before it terminates itself. The FOR loop works by executing the initialization statement only once at the beginning of the loop. The test expression is then checked against the program. If the text expression is false, the loop is terminated; but if the expression is true then the code inside the body is executed and then update expression is updated. The loop continues until the text expression becomes false.

5.6. Do While Loop

Do-while loop is an exit controlled loop i.e. the condition is checked at the end of loop. It means the statements inside do-while loop are executed at least once even if the condition is false. Do-while loop is an variant of while loop. In order to exit a do-while loop either the condition must be false or we should use break statement.

Syntax

The syntax of a **do...while** loop in C programming language is –

```
do {
  statement(s);
} while( condition );
```

Notice that the conditional expression appears at the end of the loop, so the statement(s) in the loop executes once before the condition is tested.

If the condition is true, the flow of control jumps back up to do, and the statement(s) in the loop executes again. This process repeats until the given condition becomes false.

Flow Diagram

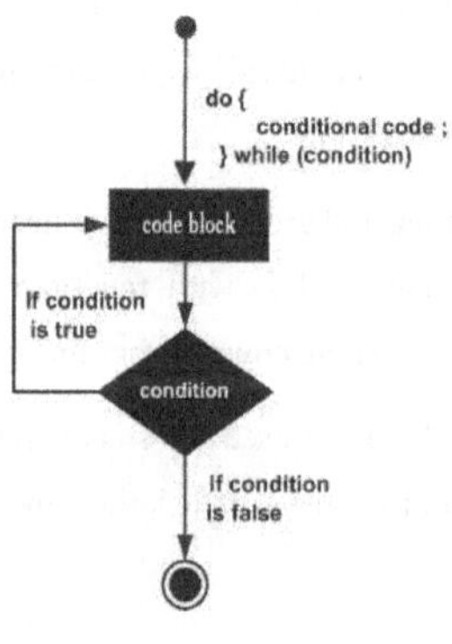

Example

```
#include<stdio.h>
int main (){
/* local variable definition */
int a =10;
/* do loop execution */
do{
   printf("value of a: %d\n", a);
   a = a +1;
}while( a <20);
return0;
}
```

When the above code is compiled and executed, it produces the following result.

```
value of a: 10
value of a: 11
value of a: 12
value of a: 13
value of a: 14
value of a: 15
value of a: 16
value of a: 17
value of a: 18
value of a: 19
```

While vs Do While

BASIS FOR COMPARISON	WHILE	DO-WHILE

General Form	while (condition) {
	statements; //body of loop
	}
		do{
		.
		statements; // body of loop.
		.
		} while(condition);

Controlling Condition	In 'while' loop the controlling condition appears at the start of the loop.	In 'do-while' loop the controlling condition appears at the end of the loop.
Iterations	The iterations do not occur if, the condition at the first iteration, appears false.	The iteration occurs at least once even if the condition is false at the first iteration.

5.7. Exercises

1) What will be the output of the C program?

```
#include<stdio.h>
int main()
{
        int i, j;
        for(i = 1, j = 1;i<=3,j<=3;i++,j++)
        printf("%d %d ",i, j);
        return 0;
}
```

A. Compilation Error

B. 1 2 3 1 2 3

C. 1 1 2 2 3 3

D. None of the above

Answer

Option: C

Explanation

Here, two for loops are embedded in a single for loop. Thus two for loops printf simultaneously and outputted 1 1 2 2 3 3.

2) What will be the output of the C program?

```
#include<stdio.h>
int main()
{
        int i = 1, j = 1;
        for(;j;printf("%d %d ",i, j))
        j = i++ <= 1;
        return 0;
}
```

A. 1 2 3 0

B. 1 1 2 2

C. 2 1 3 0

D. 0 1 2 3

Answer

Option: C

Explanation

i = 1, j = 1;

for (;j;printf("%d %d ",i, j))

Then for loop can be written as

for(;1;printf("%d %d ",i, j))

This becomes infinte for loop as the condition is always 1

now j = i++ <= 1;

ie) j = 1 <= 1;

ie) i = 2 for the every next line.

Now the control goes to the increment part and prints 2 1

still the condition in for loop is 1.

again it comes to j = i++ <= 1;

j = 2 <= 1;

here the condition is false and set j = 0;

Now the control goes to the increment part and prints 3 0.

Now the condition in for loop is 0 and terminate the for loop.

thus 2 1 3 0 is outputted.

3) What will be the output of the C program, if input is 6 for the first execution alone?

```
#include<stdio.h>
int i;
int main()
{
        int t;
        for (t=4;scanf("%d",&i)-t;printf("%d\n",i))
        printf("%d--", t--);
        return 0;
}
```

A. 4--6

B. 6--

C. 4--

D. None of the above

Answer

Option: A

Explanation

Clearly, for (t=4;scanf("%d",&i)-t;printf("%d\n",i))

for (t=4;2;printf("%d\n",i))

Now for loop condition is true and printf() statement is executed and prints 4—

Now the control goes to increment part and prints 6.

Thus 4--6 is outputted.

Note this for ends only when you enter 0 as an input.

4) What will be the output of the C program?

```
#include<stdio.h>
int main()
{
        char i = 0;
        for(;i>=0;i++);
        printf("%d\n", i);
        return 0;
}
```

A. Compilation error

B. -128

C. 0

D. 1

Answer

Option: B

Explanation

for(;i>=0;i++); compiler executes this line until it becomes falls. As i belongs to char type, for loop will exit when i = -128; because it loops from 0 to -128.

5) What will be the output of the C program?

```
#include<stdio.h>
int main()
{
        unsigned char i = 0;
        for(;i<=0;i++) ;
        printf("%d\n",i);
        return 0;
}
```

A. 127

B. 128

C. Program never ends

D. 0

Answer

Option: C

Explanation

Here, the char is declared as unsigned char. So the i++ in for loop can never yield negative value and i >= 0 never becomes false so that it loop for infinite number of times.

6) What will be the output of the C program, if input is 6?

```
#include<stdio.h>
int main()
{
        int i;
        for(i = 0; i>9; i+=3)
        {
        printf("for ");
        }
        return 0;
}
```

A. Nothing prints

B. for

C. for for for

D. None of the above

Answer

Option: A

Explanation

For loop condition fails at the first iteration itself. Thus it prints nothing.

7) What will be the output of the C program by considering 'b' as a User input?

```
#include<stdio.h>
int main()
{
        int i = 1, j = 1;
        for(--i && j++ ; i<10; i+=2)
        {
                printf("loop ");
        }
        return 0;
}
```

A. Compilation error

B. Program never ends

C. loop loop loop loop loop

D. None of the above

8) What will be the output of the C program?

```
#include<stdio.h>
int main()
{
        for(5;2;2)
        printf("Hello");
        return 0;
}
```

A. Compilation error

B. Program never ends

C. Hello

D. None of the above

Answer

Option: B

Explanation

Here in condition place of for loop, we just put a non zero value, thus it becomes infinite for loop.

9) What will be the output of the C program?

```
#include<stdio.h>
int main()
{
        static int i;
        for(i++;++i;i++)
        {
                printf("%d ", i);
                if(i == 6)
                break;
        }
        return 0;
}
```

A. 2 4

B. No output

C. 2 4 6

D. Program never ends

Answer

Option: C

Explanation

By Default, the values of static int variable is set to zero by C compiler. i.e) i = 0; Clearly, the for loop in this program is infinite for loop, ie) At first iteration the program looks like for(0;2;2) that is it 2 4 6 8 10 .. and so on. By this program we breaks when i = 6.

10) What will be the output of the C program by considering 'b' as a User input?

```
#include<stdio.h>
int main()
{
        for(;;)
        {
                printf("%d ", 10);
        }
        return 0;
}
```

A. Compilation error

B. 10

C. Program never ends

D. None of the above

Answer

Option: C

Explanation

it is infinite for loop

11) What will be the output of the C program?

```
#include<stdio.h>
int x = -1;
int main(){
        while(x++ == 1)
                printf("loop");
        return 0;
}
```

A. Prints Nothing

B. loop

C. loop loop

D. loop loop loop

Answer

Option: A

Explanation

The condition of this loop says that if x++ == 1 then executes the statement, otherwise don't. The condition is false so the control exit from the loop and program ends.

12) What will be the output of the C program?

```
#include<stdio.h>
int main(){
        int i = 5;
        while(--i > 0)
                printf("Loop ");
        return 0;
}
```

A. Loop Loop Loop Loop Loop Loop

B. Loop Loop Loop Loop Loop

C. Loop Loop Loop Loop

D. Loop Loop Loop

Answer

Option: C

Explanation

We have declared and intialize the variable i = 5, the condition is (--i > 0). Here i is pre-decremented one by one until 1. It will be 4, 3, 2 and 1 for each iteration.

13) What will be the output of the C program?

```
#include<stdio.h>
int main()
{
        while(printf("%d", 5) < 4)
                printf("Loop ");
        return 0;
}
```

A. Prints Nothing

B. 5Loop 5Loop 5Loop 5Loop 5Loop

C. 5Loop

D. Infinite iterations or Infinite Loop

Answer

Option: D

Explanation

We don't have any control in the above C program because there is no variables. If there is any variable we can control it. The condition is (printf("%d", 5) < 4) it will be (1 < 4), the condition is always true. So the loops is infinite. The same program using some variable.

14) What will be the output of the C program?

```
#include<stdio.h>
int main()
{
        int i = 0;
        while(i < 4, 5)
        {
                printf("Loop ");
```

```
            i++;
        }
        return 0;
}
```

A. Infinite Loop

B. Loop Loop Loop Loop Loop

C. Loop Loop Loop Loop

D. Prints Nothing

Answer

Option: A

Explanation

The above while loop have a condition while(i < 4, 5) it is in the format of while (expression1, expression2), here it is separated by a comma (,) operator, so the expression1 is evaluated first then expression2 is evaluated, though expression1 is failed, expression2 will execute until the expression2 becomes false.

15) What will be the output of the C program?

```
#include<stdio.h>
int main()
{
        int i;
        while(0, i < 4)
        {
            printf("Loop ");
            i++;
        }
        return 0;
}
```

A. Prints Nothing

B. Infinite Loop

C. Loop Loop Loop Loop

D. Loop Loop Loop Loop Loop

Answer

Option: C

Explanation

The condition (0, i < 4) is in the format (expression1, expression2), here expression1 (0) goes false, though expression2 will get executed until expression2 is false.

16) What will be the output of the C program?

```
#include<stdio.h>
int main()
{
        int i = 0;
        while(i < 3, i = 0, i < 5)
        {
                printf("Loop ");
                i++;
        }
    return 0;
}
```

A. Loop Loop Loop Loop Loop

B. Infinite Loop

C. Loop Loop Loop

D. Prints Nothing

Answer

Option: B

Explanation

The while loop have a condition (i < 3, i = 0, i < 5) is in a format (expression1, expression2, expression3). In each iteration the compiler checks each expression.

In this program, the loop will be:

Iteration 1: 0 < 3, 0, 0 < 5

Iteration 2: 1 < 3, 0, 0 < 5

Iteration 3: 1 < 3, 0, 0 < 5

Iteration 4: 1 < 3, 0, 0 < 5

The loop continues as infinite because i is initialized to 0 each time.

17) What will be the output of the C program?

```
#include<stdio.h>
int main()
{
        int i == 4, j == 7;
        while(++i < --j)
                printf("Loop")
        return 0;
}
```

A. Loop

B. Loop Loop

C. Loop Loop Loop

D. Infinite Loop

Answer

Option: A

Explanation

The while(--i == --j) is (5 < 6), so the statement inside the loop will executes once, if we go for another iteration the condition will be wrong.

18) What will be the output of the C program?

```
#include<stdio.h>
int main()
{
        int i = 0;
        while(i++)
        {
                printf("Loop ");
                if(i == 3)
                        break;
        }
return 0;
}
```

A. Loop

B. Loop Loop Loop

C. Loop Loop Loop Loop

D. Prints Nothing

Answer

Option: D

Explanation

The condition is while(i++), the expression is post incremented variable. So when it is applied for first time the condition will be False because while(0).

19) What will be the output of the C program?

```
#include<stdio.h>
#define NULL 0
int main()
{
        while (NULL == 0)
        {
                printf("Loop");
                break;
        }
        return 0;
}
```

A. Prints Nothing

B. Loop

C. Loop Loop

D. Compilation Error

Answer

Option: B

Explanation

The condition is true so it returns 1 and executes the block only once.

20) What will be the output of the C program?

```
#include<stdio.h>
int main(){
        int i = 4;
        while(i == 4--)
                printf("Loop ");
        return 0;
}
```

A. Loop Loop Loop Loop

B. Loop Loop loop

C. Compilation Error

D. Prints Nothing

Answer

Option: C

Explanation

Compilation Error: Lvalue required we can't use pre or post increment operator with constants or Literal values. So it will raise an error at compile time.

Try by Yourself

1) What will be the output of the C program?

```
#include<stdio.h>
int main()
{
        int fun = {
        printf("C for loop ")
        };
        int x = 5;
        for(x=0;x<=fun;x++)
        {
        printf("%x ", x);
        }
        return 0;
}
```

A. 0 1 2 3 4 5 6 7 8 9

B. C for loop 0 1 2 3 4 5 6 7 8 9 a

C. 0 1 2 3 4 5 6 7 8 9 a

D. None of the above

2) What will be the output of the C program?

```
#include<stdio.h>
int main()
{
        int i;
        for(i = 0;i<=3;i++);
        printf("%d", i);
        return 0;
}
```

A. Compilation error

B. 1 2 3

C. 4

D. 0 1 2 3

3) What will be the output of the C program?

```
#include<stdio.h>
int main()
{
        char i = 0;
        for(;i++;printf("%d", i)) ;
        printf("%d",i);
        return 0;
}
```

A. Compilation error

B. 0

C. 1

D. Program never ends

4) What will be the output of the C program, if input is 6?

```
#include<stdio.h>
int main()
{
        int i = 0;
        for(i = 0;i == 0;i++)
        {
                printf("%d", i);
        }
return 0;
}
```

A. 0

B. Nothing prints

C. 1

D. None of the above

5) What will be the output of the C program by considering 'b' as a User input?

```
#include<stdio.h>
int main()
{
        int i;
        for(i = 0;i<(i++, 5);i++)
                printf("%d ",i);
        return 0;
}
```

A. 1 3 5

B. 1 2 3 4 5

C. 1 3

D. None of the above

6) What will be the output of the C program?

```
#include<stdio.h>
int main()
{
        int i;
        for(i = 0;i<0,5;i++)
                printf("%d\n",i);
        return 0;
}
```

A. 1 3

B. Program never ends

C. 1 3 5

D. None of the above

7) What will be the output of the C program?

```
#include<stdio.h>
int main()
{
        int i, j;
        for(i = 0, j=5;i<j;i++,j--)
                printf("%d %d ",i, j);
        return 0;
}
```

A. 0 1 2 5 4 3

B. Compilation error

C. 0 5 1 4 2 3

D. Runtime error

8) What will be the output of the C program?

```
#include<stdio.h>
int main()
{
        int i = 1;
        while(printf("%d", 5) == 1 == i)
        {
                printf("SuperLoop ");
        }
        return 0;
}
```

A. 5Super Loop

B. Prints Nothing

C. 5 SuperLoop 5SuperLoop 5SuperLoop 5SuperLoop 5SuperLoop

D. Infinite Times

9) What will be the output of the C program?

```
#include<stdio.h>
int main()
{
        int i;
        while(sizeof(NULL))
        {
                printf("inside loop");
                continue;
                break;
        }
        return 0;
}
```

A. Infinite Loop

B. inside loop

C. inside loop inside loop

D. Compilation Error

10) What will be the output of the C program?

```
#include<stdio.h>
int main(){
        while(sizeof(0))
        {
                printf("Loop ");
                if(sizeof(0))
                break;
                else
                continue;
        }
        return 0;
}
```

A. Error

B. Infinite Loop

C. Loop Loop

D. Loop

11) What will be the output of the C program?

```
#include<stdio.h>
int main()
{
        int i = 5, j = 0;
        while(i - j)
                printf("HaiLoop");
        return 0;
}
```

A. HaiLoop HaiLoop HaiLoop

B. HaiLoop HaiLoop HaiLoop HaiLoop HaiLoop

C. HaiLoop HaiLoop

D. Infinite Loop

12) What will be the output of the C program ?

```
#include<stdio.h>
int main(){
	float ft = 7.5;
	while(ft)
	{
		printf("Loop");
		ft = ft - .5;
		if(ft == 5.0f)
			break;
	}
	return 0;
}
```

A. Prints Nothing

B. Looop

C. Loop Loop Loop Loop Loop

D. Compilation Error

13) What will be the output of the C program?

```
#include<stdio.h>
int main()
{
	int i = 0;
	while(;;)
	{
		printf("Hai Loop");
		if (i == 2)
		break;
		i++;
	}
	return 0;
}
```

A. Hai Loop

B. Compilation Error

C. Hai Loop Hai Loop

D. Hai Loop Hai Loop Hai Loop

14) What will be the output of the C program?

```
#include<stdio.h>
int main()
{
        while(!!7)
                printf("Hai");
        return 0;
}
```

A. Hai Hai Hai Hai Hai Hai Hai

B. Hai

C. Infinite Loop

D. Prints Nothing

15) What will be the output of the C program?

```
#include<stdio.h>
int main(){
        int i = -1;
        do
        {
                printf("HiDoWhile ");
        }while(i++);
        return 0;
}
```

A. Compilation Error

B. HiDoWhile

C. HiDoWhile HiDoWhile HiDoWhile

D. HiDoWhile HiDoWhile

16) What will be the output of the C program?

```
#include<stdio.h>
int main(){
        while(!printf("Steve is awesome"));
        return 0;
}
```

A. Steve is awesome

B. Infinite Loop

C. Prints Nothing

D. None of the Above

Answers

1) b 2)c 3)c 4)a 5)c 6)b 7)c 8)d 9)a 10)d 11)b 12)c 13)b 14)c 15)d 16)a

CHAPTER 6

ARRAYS

6.1. Introduction

Arrays a kind of data structure that can store a fixed-size sequential collection of elements of the same type. An array is used to store a collection of data, but it is often more useful to think of an array as a collection of variables of the same type.

Instead of declaring individual variables, such as number0, number1, ..., and number99, you declare one array variable such as numbers and use numbers[0], numbers[1], and ..., numbers[99] to represent individual variables. A specific element in an array is accessed by an index.

All arrays consist of contiguous memory locations. The lowest address corresponds to the first element and the highest address to the last element.

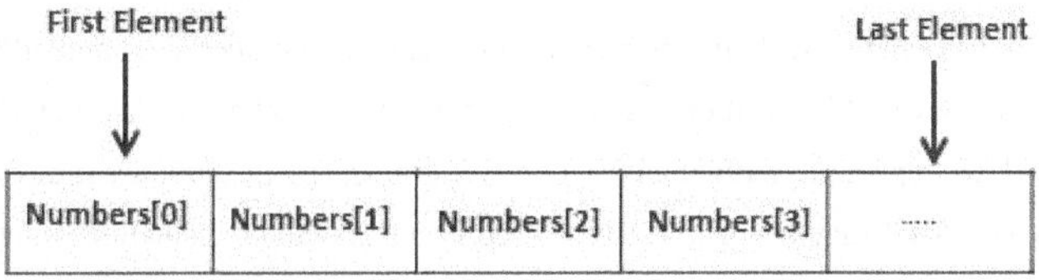

6.2. Why We Need Array?

Consider a situation where we need to store five integer numbers. If we use programming's simple variable and data type concepts, then we need five variables of **int** data type and the program will be as follows.

```
#include<stdio.h>
int main(){
int number1;
int number2;
int number3;
int number4;
int number5;
  number1 =10;
  number2 =20;
  number3 =30;
```

```
  number4 =40;
  number5 =50;
  printf("number1: %d\n", number1);
  printf("number2: %d\n", number2);
  printf("number3: %d\n", number3);
  printf("number4: %d\n", number4);
  printf("number5: %d\n", number5);
}
```

It was simple, because we had to store just five integer numbers. Now let's assume we have to store 5000 integer numbers. Are we going to use 5000 variables?

To handle such situations, almost all the programming languages provide a concept called **array**. An array is a data structure, which can store a fixed-size collection of elements of the same data type. An array is used to store a collection of data, but it is often more useful to think of an array as a collection of variables of the same type.

Instead of declaring individual variables, such as number1, number2, ..., number99, you just declare one array variable **number** of integer type and use number1[0], number1[1], and ..., number1[99] to represent individual variables. Here, 0, 1, 2, ...99 are **index** associated with **var** variable and they are being used to represent individual elements available in the array.

6.3. Create, Initialize and Accessing Arrays

Create Arrays

To create an array variable in C, a programmer specifies the type of the elements and the number of elements to be stored in that array. Given below is a simple syntax to create an array in C programming.

```
type arrayName [ arraySize ];
```

This is called a *single-dimensional* array. The **arraySize** must be an integer constant greater than zero and **type** can be any valid C data type. For example, now to declare a 10-element array called **number** of type **int**, use this statement.

```
int number[10];
```

Here, *number* is a variable array, which is sufficient to hold up to 10 integer numbers.

Initializing Arrays

You can initialize an array in C either one by one or using a single statement as follows.

```
int number[5] = {10, 20, 30, 40, 50};
```

The number of values between braces { } cannot be larger than the number of elements that we declare for the array between square brackets [ ].

If you omit the size of the array, an array just big enough to hold the initialization is created. Therefore, if you write.

```
int number[] = {10, 20, 30, 40, 50};
```

You will create exactly the same array as you did in the previous example. Following is an example to assign a single element of the array.

```
number[4] = 50;
```

The above statement assigns element number 5th in the array with a value of 50. All arrays have 0 as the index of their first element which is also called the base index and the last index of an array will be the total size of the array minus 1. The following image shows the pictorial representation of the array we discussed above.

Index	0	1	2	3	4
number	10	20	30	40	50

Accessing Array Elements

An element is accessed by indexing the array name. This is done by placing the index of the element within square brackets after the name of the array. For example.

```
int var = number[9];
```

The above statement will take the 10th element from the array and assign the value to **var** variable. The following example uses all the above-mentioned three concepts viz. creation, assignment, and accessing arrays.

```
#include<stdio.h>
int main (){
int number[10];/* number is an array of 10 integers */
int i =0;
```

```
/* Initialize elements of array n to 0 */
while( i <10){
/* Set element at location i to i + 100 */
    number[ i ]= i +100;
    i = i +1;
}
/* Output each array element's value */
  i =0;
while( i <10){
    printf("number[%d] = %d\n", i, number[i]);
    i = i +1;
}
return0;
}
```

When the above code is compiled and executed, it produces the following result.

```
number[0] = 100
number[1] = 101
number[2] = 102
number[3] = 103
number[4] = 104
number[5] = 105
number[6] = 106
number[7] = 107
number[8] = 108
number[9] = 109
```

How to insert and print array elements?

```
int mark[5] = {19, 10, 8, 17, 9}
// insert different value to third element
mark[3] = 9;
// take input from the user and insert in third element
scanf("%d", &mark[2]);
// take input from the user and insert in (i+1)th element
scanf("%d", &mark[i]);
```

```
// print first element of an array
printf("%d", mark[0]);
// print ith element of an array
printf("%d", mark[i-1]);
```

Arrays are of two types:

1. One-dimensional arrays.
2. Two Dimensional.
3. Multidimensional arrays.

Example

```
// Program to find the average of n (n < 10) numbers using arrays
#include<stdio.h>
int main()
{
int marks[10], i, n, sum =0, average;
   printf("Enter n: ");
   scanf("%d",&n);
for(i=0; i<n;++i)
{
      printf("Enter number%d: ",i+1);
      scanf("%d",&marks[i]);
      sum += marks[i];
}
   average = sum/n;
   printf("Average = %d", average);
return0;
}
```

Output

```
Enter n: 5
Enter number1: 45
```

```
Enter number2: 35
Enter number3: 38
Enter number4: 31
Enter number5: 49
Average = 39
```

6.4. Two Dimensional Array

The simplest form of multidimensional array is the two-dimensional array. A two-dimensional array is, in essence, a list of one-dimensional arrays. To declare a two-dimensional integer array of size [x][y], you would write something as follows.

```
type arrayName [ x ][ y ];
```

Where **type** can be any valid C data type and **arrayName** will be a valid C identifier. A two-dimensional array can be considered as a table which will have x number of rows and y number of columns. A two-dimensional array **a**, which contains three rows and four columns can be shown as follows

	Column 0	Column 1	Column 2	Column 3
Row 0	a[0][0]	a[0][1]	a[0][2]	a[0][3]
Row 1	a[1][0]	a[1][1]	a[1][2]	a[1][3]
Row 2	a[2][0]	a[2][1]	a[2][2]	a[2][3]

Thus, every element in the array **a** is identified by an element name of the form **a[i][j]**, where 'a' is the name of the array, and 'i' and 'j' are the subscripts that uniquely identify each element in 'a'.

Initializing Two-Dimensional Arrays

Multidimensional arrays may be initialized by specifying bracketed values for each row. Following is an array with 3 rows and each row has 4 columns.

```
int a[3][4]={
{0,1,2,3},/* initializers for row indexed by 0 */
{4,5,6,7},/* initializers for row indexed by 1 */
```

```
{8,9,10,11}/* initializers for row indexed by 2 */
};
```

The nested braces, which indicate the intended row, are optional. The following initialization is equivalent to the previous example.

```
int a[3][4] = {0,1,2,3,4,5,6,7,8,9,10,11};
```

Things that you Must Consider While Initializing a 2D Array

We already know, when we initialize a normal array (or you can say one dimensional array) during declaration, we need not to specify the size of it. However that's not the case with 2D array, you must always specify the second dimension even if you are specifying elements during the declaration. Let's understand this with the help of few examples –

```
/* Valid declaration*/
int abc[2][2]={1,2,3,4}
/* Valid declaration*/
int abc[][2]={1,2,3,4}
/* Invalid declaration - you must specify second dimension*/
int abc[][]={1,2,3,4}
/* Invalid because of the same reason  mentioned above*/
int abc[2][]={1,2,3,4}
```

Accessing Two-Dimensional Array Elements

An element in a two-dimensional array is accessed by using the subscripts, i.e., row index and column index of the array. For example.

```
int val = a[2][3];
```

The above statement will take the 4th element from the 3rd row of the array. You can verify it in the above figure. Let us check the following program where we have used a nested loop to handle a two-dimensional array.

```
#include<stdio.h>
int main (){
/* an array with 5 rows and 2 columns*/
int a[5][2]={{0,0},{1,2},{2,4},{3,6},{4,8}};
int i, j;
```

```
/* output each array element's value */
for( i =0; i <5; i++){
for( j =0; j <2; j++){
     printf("a[%d][%d] = %d\n", i,j, a[i][j]);
}
}
return0;
}
```

When the above code is compiled and executed, it produces the following result –

```
a[0][0]: 0
a[0][1]: 0
a[1][0]: 1
a[1][1]: 2
a[2][0]: 2
a[2][1]: 4
a[3][0]: 3
a[3][1]: 6
a[4][0]: 4
a[4][1]: 8
```

As explained above, you can have arrays with any number of dimensions, although it is likely that most of the arrays you create will be of one or two dimensions.

Example

```
#include<stdio.h>
int main(){
  /* 2D array declaration*/
  int disp[2][3];
  /*Counter variables for the loop*/
  int i, j;
  for(i=0; i<2; i++) {
    for(j=0;j<3;j++) {
      printf("Enter value for disp[%d][%d]:", i, j);
      scanf("%d", &disp[i][j]);
    }
```

```
    }
    //Displaying array elements
    printf("Two Dimensional array elements:\n");
    for(i=0; i<2; i++) {
      for(j=0;j<3;j++) {
        printf("%d ", disp[i][j]);
        if(j==2){
          printf("\n");
        }
      }
    }
    return 0;
}
```

Output

```
Enter value for disp[0][0]:1

Enter value for disp[0][1]:2

Enter value for disp[0][2]:3

Enter value for disp[1][0]:4

Enter value for disp[1][1]:5

Enter value for disp[1][2]:6

Two Dimensional array elements:

1 2 3

4 5 6
```

6.5. Multidimensional Array

In C, we can define multidimensional arrays in simple words as array of arrays. Data in multidimensional arrays are stored in tabular form (in row major order).

General form of declaring N-dimensional arrays:

data_type array_name[size1][size2]....[sizeN];
data_type: Type of data to be stored in the array.

Here data_type is valid C data type

array_name: Name of the array

size1, size2,... ,sizeN: Sizes of the dimensions

How to Declare a Multidimensional Array in C

A multidimensional array is declared using the following syntax:

type array_name[d1][d2][d3][d4].........[dn];

Where each **d** is a dimension, and **dn** is the size of final dimension.

Examples

1. **int table[5][5][20];**
2. **float arr[5][6][5][6][5];**

In Example 1

- **int** designates the array type integer.
- **table** is the name of our 3D array.
- Our array can hold 500 integer-type elements. This number is reached by multiplying the value of each dimension. In this case: **5x5x20=500**.

In Example 2

- Array **arr** is a five-dimensional array.
- It can hold 4500 floating-point elements (**5x6x5x6x5=4500**).

Can you see the power of declaring an array over variables? When it comes to holding multiple values in C programming, we would need to declare several variables. But a single array can hold thousands of values.

Note: For the sake of simplicity, this book discusses 3D arrays only. Once you grab the logic of how the 3D array works then you can handle 4D arrays and larger.

Explanation of a 3D Array

Let's take a closer look at a 3D array. A 3D array is essentially an array of arrays of arrays: it's an array or collection of 2D arrays, and a 2D array is an array of 1D array.

It may sound a bit confusing, but don't worry. As you practice working with multidimensional arrays, you start to grasp the logic. The diagram below may help you understand:

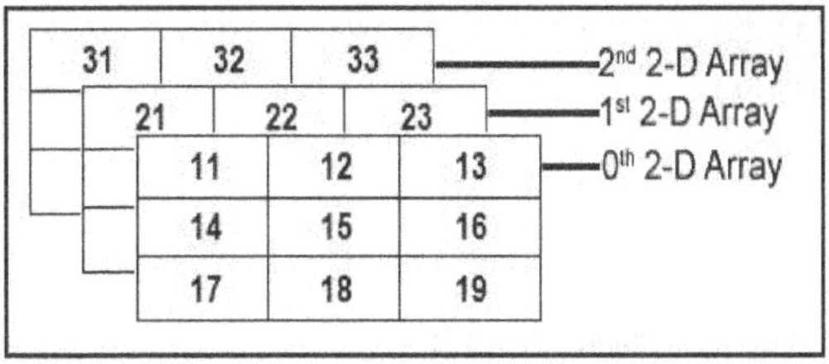

Size of Multidimensional Arrays

Total number of elements that can be stored in a multidimensional array can be calculated by multiplying the size of all the dimensions. For example: The array int x[10][20] can store total (10*20) = 200 elements. Similarly array int x[5][10][20] can store total (5*10*20) = 1000 elements.

Initializing a 3D Array in C

Like any other variable or array, a 3D array can be initialized at the time of compilation. By default, in C, an uninitialized 3D array contains "garbage" values, not valid for the intended use.

Let's see a complete example on how to initialize a 3D array.

```
#include<stdio.h>
#include<conio.h>
void main()
{
int i, j, k;
int arr[3][3][3]=
    {
      {
      {11, 12, 13},
      {14, 15, 16},
      {17, 18, 19}
      },
      {
      {21, 22, 23},
      {24, 25, 26},
      {27, 28, 29}
      },
      {
```

```
                {31, 32, 33},
                {34, 35, 36},
                {37, 38, 39}
                },      };
        clrscr();
        printf(":::3D Array Elements:::\n\n");
        for(i=0;i<3;i++)
        {
          for(j=0;j<3;j++)
          {
            for(k=0;k<3;k++)
            {
            printf("%d\t",arr[i][j][k]);
            }
            printf("\n");
          }
          printf("\n");
        }
        getch();
}
```

Example

```
#include <stdio.h>
int main()
{
  int a[10][10], b[10][10], result[10][10], r1, c1, r2, c2, i, j, k;
  printf("Enter rows and column for first matrix: ");
  scanf("%d %d", &r1, &c1);
  printf("Enter rows and column for second matrix: ");
  scanf("%d %d",&r2, &c2);
  // Column of first matrix should be equal to column of second matrix and
  while (c1 != r2)
  {
    printf("Error! column of first matrix not equal to row of second.\n\n");
    printf("Enter rows and column for first matrix: ");
```

```
    scanf("%d %d", &r1, &c1);
    printf("Enter rows and column for second matrix: ");
    scanf("%d %d",&r2, &c2);
}
// Storing elements of first matrix.
printf("\nEnter elements of matrix 1:\n");
for(i=0; i<r1; ++i)
    for(j=0; j<c1; ++j)
    {
        printf("Enter elements a%d%d: ",i+1, j+1);
        scanf("%d", &a[i][j]);
    }
// Storing elements of second matrix.
printf("\nEnter elements of matrix 2:\n");
for(i=0; i<r2; ++i)
    for(j=0; j<c2; ++j)
    {
        printf("Enter elements b%d%d: ",i+1, j+1);
        scanf("%d",&b[i][j]);
    }
// Initializing all elements of result matrix to 0
for(i=0; i<r1; ++i)
    for(j=0; j<c2; ++j)
    {
        result[i][j] = 0;
    }
// Multiplying matrices a and b and
// storing result in result matrix
for(i=0; i<r1; ++i)
    for(j=0; j<c2; ++j)
        for(k=0; k<c1; ++k)
        {
            result[i][j]+=a[i][k]*b[k][j];
        }
```

```
    // Displaying the result
    printf("\nOutput Matrix:\n");
    for(i=0; i<r1; ++i)
        for(j=0; j<c2; ++j)
        {
            printf("%d  ", result[i][j]);
            if(j == c2-1)
                printf("\n\n");
        }
    return 0;
}
```

Output

```
Enter rows and column for first matrix: 3
2
Enter rows and column for second matrix: 3
2
Error! column of first matrix not equal to row of second.
Enter rows and column for first matrix: 2
3
Enter rows and column for second matrix: 3
2
Enter elements of matrix 1:
Enter elements a11: 3
Enter elements a12: -2
Enter elements a13: 5
Enter elements a21: 3
Enter elements a22: 0
Enter elements a23: 4
Enter elements of matrix 2:
Enter elements b11: 2
Enter elements b12: 3
```

```
Enter elements b21: -9

Enter elements b22: 0

Enter elements b31: 0

Enter elements b32: 4

Output Matrix:

24 29

6 25
```

6.6. Exercises

1) What will be the output of the C program by considering 'b' as a User input?

```
#include<stdio.h>
int main()
{
        char temp;
        char arr[10] = {1, 2, 3, 4, 5, 6, 9, 8};
        temp = (arr + 1)[2];
        printf("%d\n", temp);
        return 0;
}
```

A. 2
B. 3
C. 4
D. 5

Answer

Option: C

Explanation

Here, temp = (arr + 1)[2];

Let us consider the address of first element in an array arr[10] is 2293416 then temp looks like this temp = (2293416 + 1)[2];

Now temp =(2293420)[2];, which denotes temp = "index value of 2 from the address 2293420(value = 2)";

Now temp = 4;(address = 2293428)

Thus the program outputted 4.

2) What will be the output of the C program?

```
#include<stdio.h>
int main()
{
        int arr[5][5][5] = {0};
        printf("%d", ( &arr+1 - &arr ));
        return 0;
}
```

A. 0

B. Compilation error

C. 1

D. 4

Answer

Option: C

Explanation

printf("%d", (&arr+1 - &arr)); let us consider the address of an array arr starts from 2293420

Then, printf ("%d", (2293420 +1 - 2293420);

printf("%d", 0 + 1);

printf("%d", 1);

Thus 1 is outputted.

3) What will be the output of the C program, if input is 6?

```
#include<stdio.h>
```

```
void fun(int[][3]);
int main(void)
{
        int arr[3][3] = { {1, 2, 3}, {4, 5, 6}, {7, 8, 9} };
        fun(arr);
        printf("%d\n", arr[2][1]);
        return 0;
}
void fun(int b[][3])
{
        ++b;
        b[1][1] = 15;
}
```

A. 15

B. 9

C. 8

D. 7

Answer

Option: A

Explanation

This question from 2braces.com is more tricky.

Fun(arr) returns the address of first element in an array to the function void fun();

LET us consider the address of the values in arr[3][3] is 2293420.

When it passes through the function void fun(int b[][3]), its value is pre-incremented ++b. As it is a multi dimensional array ++b will not skip the address next to the last value in an array arr[][3] instead it skip the address next to first part only i.e) now b[][3] array starts with the address 2293432 (i.e) starts from the value 4 but index from 0.

Clearly b[0][0] = 4

Now b[1][1] = 15 will affect the value 8 in arr of array.

Thus arr[2][1] outputted 15.

4) What will be the output of the C program by considering 'b' as a User input?

```
#include<stdio.h>
int main(){
        int rows = 3, colums = 4, i, j, k;
        int a[3][4] = {1, 2, 3, 5, 7};
        i = j = k = 00;
        for(i = 0;i<rows;i++)
        for(j = 0;j<colums;j++)
        if(a[k][j]<k)
        k = a[i][j];
        printf("%d\n", k);
        return 0;
}
```

A. 00

B. No output

C. 0

D. 7

Answer

Option: C

Explanation

Initially we set i = 0, j = 0, k = 0. zero be never greater than any integer values in an array a[3][4], thus if condition fails. and 0 is outputted.

5) What will be the output of the C program?

```
#include<stdio.h>
int main()
{
        int i = 0;
        printf("Hello");
        char s[4] = {'\b', '\t', '\r', '\n'};
        for(i = 0;i<4;i++){
```

```
        printf("%c", s[i]);
}
return 0;
}
```

A. Hello

B. Compilation error

C. Hell

D. None of the above

Answer

Option: C

Explanation

Hello is printed followed by \b\t\r\n.

i.e) Hello\b\t\r\n.

i.e) Hell\t\r\n.

i.e) Hell   \r\n.

i.e) Hell\n.

i.e) Hell is Outputted.

6) What will be the output of the C program?

```
#include<stdio.h>
int main()
{
        int i = 0;
        char s[4] = {'\0', '\0', '\0', '\0'};
        for(i = 0;i<4;i++)
        {
                printf("%c", s[i]);
        }
```

```
        return 0;
}
```

A. \0 \0 \0

B. \0 \0 \0 \0

C. No output

D. None of the above

Answer

Option: C

Explanation

\0 = NULL. Thus compiler prints nothing.

Try By Yourself

1) What will be the output of the C program?

```
#include<stdio.h>
int main()
{
        int i = 0;
        printf("Hello");
        char s[4] = {'\b', '\r', '\t', '\n'};
        for(i = 0;i<4;i++)
        {
                printf("%c", s[i]);
        }
        return 0;
}
```

A. No output

B. Hell

C. Hello

D. Compilation error

2) What will be the output of the C program?

```
#include<stdio.h>
```

```
int main()
{
        int arr[2] = {1, 2, 3, 4, 5};
        printf("%d", arr[3]);
        return 0;
}
```

A. 3

B. 4

C. Some Garbage value

D. Compilation error

3) What will be the output of the C program?

```
#include<stdio.h>
int main()
{
        int a, b, c;
        int arr[5] = {1, 2, 3, 25, 7};
        a = ++arr[1];
        b = arr[1]++;
        c = arr[a++];
        printf("%d--%d--%d", a, b, c);
        return 0;
}
```

A. 4--3--25

B. 3--3--25

C. 4--4--25

D. 3--4--25

4) What will be the output of the C program?

```
#include<stdio.h>
#define arr[5] {1, 2, 3, 4, 5}
int main()
{
        printf("%d", arr[1]);
        return 0;
}
```

A. 1

B. 2

C. Compilation error

D. Runtime error

5) What will be the output of the C program?

```
#include<stdio.h>
int main()
{
        int arr[1] = {2};
        printf("%d", 0[arr]);
        return 0;
}
```

A. Compilation error

B. Some Garbage value

C. 0

D. 2

6) What will be the output of the C program?

```
#include<stdio.h>
int main()
{
        int arr[3], i = 0;
        while(i < 3)
        {
                arr[i] = ++i;
        }
        for(i=0; i<3; i++)
        {
                printf("%d--", arr[i]);
        }
return 0;
}
```

A. Compilation error

B. 1--2--3--

C. Garbage value--1--2--

D. None of the above

Answers

1)a 2)c 3)c 4)c 5)d 6)c

CHAPTER 7

FUNCTION IN C

7.1. Introduction

A function is a group of statements that together perform a task. Every C program has at least one function, which is **main()**, and all the most trivial programs can define additional functions.

You can divide up your code into separate functions. How you divide up your code among different functions is up to you, but logically the division is such that each function performs a specific task.

A function **declaration** tells the compiler about a function's name, return type, and parameters. A function **definition** provides the actual body of the function.

The C standard library provides numerous built-in functions that your program can call. For example, **strcat()** to concatenate two strings, **memcpy()** to copy one memory location to another location, and many more functions.

A function can also be referred as a method or a sub-routine or a procedure, etc.

Uses of C Functions

- C functions are used to avoid rewriting same logic/code again and again in a program.
- There is no limit in calling C functions to make use of same functionality wherever required.
- We can call functions any number of times in a program and from any place in a program.
- A large C program can easily be tracked when it is divided into functions.
- The core concept of C functions are, re-usability, dividing a big task into small pieces to achieve the functionality and to improve understandability of very large C programs.

7.2. Types of Functions

1) **Predefined standard library functions** – such as puts(), gets(), printf(), scanf() etc – These are the functions which already have a definition in header files (.h files like stdio.h), so we just call them whenever there is a need to use them.
2) **User Defined functions –** The functions that we create in a program are known as user defined functions.

Why We Need Functions in C

Functions are used because of following reasons.

a) To improve the readability of code.

b) Improves the reusability of the code, same function can be used in any program rather than writing the same code from scratch.

c) Debugging of the code would be easier if you use functions, as errors are easy to be traced.

d) Reduces the size of the code, duplicate set of statements are replaced by function calls.

Syntax of a Function

```
return_type function_name (argument list)
{
Set of statements -Block of code
}
```

return_type: Return type can be of any data type such as int, double, char, void, short etc. Don't worry you will understand these terms better once you go through the examples below.

function_name: It can be anything, however it is advised to have a meaningful name for the functions so that it would be easy to understand the purpose of function just by seeing it's name.

Argument list: Argument list contains variables names along with their data types. These arguments are kind of inputs for the function. For example - A function which is used to add two integer variables, will be having two integer argument.

Block of code: Set of C statements, which will be executed whenever a call will be made to the function.

Let's split the problem so that it would be easy to understand - Function will add the two numbers so it should have some meaningful name like sum, addition, etc. For example lets take the name addition for this function.

return_type addition(argument list)

This function addition adds two integer variables, which means I need two integer variable as input, lets provide two integer parameters in the function signature. The function signature would be,

return_type addition(int num1,int num2)

The result of the sum of two integers would be integer only. Hence function should return an integer value – **I got my return type** – It would be integer.

```
int addition(int num1,int num2);
```

So you got your function prototype or signature. Now you can implement the logic in C program like this:

How to Call a Function in C?

Consider the following C program

Example1: Creating a user defined function addition()

```
#include<stdio.h>
int addition(int num1,int num2)
{
int sum;
/* Arguments are used here*/
   sum = num1+num2;
/* Function return type is integer so we are returning
    * an integer value, the sum of the passed numbers.
    */
return sum;
}
int main()
{
int var1, var2;
   printf("Enter number 1: ");
   scanf("%d",&var1);
   printf("Enter number 2: ");
   scanf("%d",&var2);
/* Calling the function here, the function return type
    * is integer so we need an integer variable to hold the
    * returned value of this function.
    */
int res = addition(var1, var2);
   printf ("Output: %d", res);
return0;
```

```
}
Output:
Enter number 1:100
Enter number 2:120
Output:220
```

Example 2: Creating a void user defined function that doesn't return anything

```
#include<stdio.h>
/* function return type is void and it doesn't have parameters*/
void introduction()
{
  printf("Hi\n");
  printf("My name is Chaitanya\n");
  printf("How are you?");
/* There is no return statement inside this function, since its
   * return type is void
   */
}
int main()
{
/*calling function*/
   introduction();
return0;
}
Output:
Hi
My name isChaitanya
How are you?
```

Few Points to Note regarding Functions in C

1) main() in C program is also a function.
2) Each C program must have at least one function, which is main().
3) There is no limit on number of functions; A C program can have any number of functions.

4) A function can call itself and it is known as "**Recursion**". I have written a separate guide for it.

C Functions Terminologies that you must remember return type: Data type of returned value. It can be void also, in such case function doesn't return any value.

Note: for example, if function return type is **char,** then function should return a value of char type and while calling this function the main() function should have a variable of char data type to store the returned value.

Structure would look like –

```
char abc(char ch1,char ch2)
{
char ch3;
...
...
return ch3;
}
int main()
{
...
char c1 = abc('a','x');
...
}
```

7.3. Call by Value vs Call by Reference

1) **Function - Call by value method** – In the call by value method the actual arguments are copied to the formal arguments, hence any operation performed by function on arguments doesn't affect actual parameters.
2) **Function - Call by reference method** – Unlike call by value, in this method, address of actual arguments (or parameters) is passed to the formal parameters, which means any operation performed on formal parameters affects the value of actual parameters.

Function call by value is the default way of calling a function in C programming. Before we discuss function call by value, lets understand the terminologies that we will use while explaining this:

Actual parameters: The parameters that appear in function calls.

Formal parameters: The parameters that appear in function declarations.

For Example

```
#include <stdio.h>
int sum(int a, int b)
{
    int c=a+b;
    return c;
}
int main(
{
   int var1 =10;
   int var2 = 20;
   int var3 = sum(var1, var2);
   printf("%d", var3);
   return 0;
}
```

In the above example variable a and b are the formal parameters (or formal arguments). Variable var1 and var2 are the actual arguments (or actual parameters). The actual parameters can also be the values. Like sum(10, 20), here 10 and 20 are actual parameters.

In this guide, we will discuss **function call by value**. If you want to read call by reference method then refer this guide: function call by reference.

Lets get back to the point.

What is Function Call By Value?

When we pass the actual parameters while calling a function then this is known as function call by value. In this case the values of actual parameters are copied to the formal parameters. Thus operations performed on the formal parameters don't reflect in the actual parameters.

Example of Function Call by Value

As mentioned above, in the call by value the actual arguments are copied to the formal arguments, hence any operation performed by function on arguments doesn't affect actual parameters. Lets take an example to understand this:

```
#include<stdio.h>
int increment(intvar)
{
```

```
var=var+1;
returnvar;
}
int main()
{
int num1=20;
int num2 = increment(num1);
  printf("num1 value is: %d", num1);
  printf("\nnum2 value is: %d", num2);
return0;
}
Output:
num1 value is:20
num2 value is:21
```

Explanation

We passed the variable num1 while calling the method, but since we are calling the function using call by value method, only the value of num1 is copied to the formal parameter var. Thus change made to the var doesn't reflect in the num1.

Example 2: Swapping Numbers Using Function Call by Value

```
#include<stdio.h>
void swapnum(int var1,int var2 )
{
int tempnum ;
/*Copying var1 value into temporary variable */
  tempnum = var1 ;
/* Copying var2 value into var1*/
  var1 = var2 ;

/*Copying temporary variable value into var2 */
  var2 = tempnum ;
}
int main()
{
```

```
int num1 =35, num2 =45;
  printf("Before swapping: %d, %d", num1, num2);
/*calling swap function*/
  swapnum(num1, num2);
  printf("\nAfter swapping: %d, %d", num1, num2);
}
```

Output

```
Before swapping: 35, 45
After swapping: 35, 45
```

Why Variables Remain Unchanged Even After the Swap?

The reason is same – function is called by value for num1 & num2. So actually var1 and var2 gets swapped (not num1 & num2). As in call by value actual parameters are just copied into the formal parameters.

Before we discuss function call by reference, lets understand the terminologies that we will use while explaining this:

Actual parameters: The parameters that appear in function calls.

Formal parameters: The parameters that appear in function declarations.

For example: We have a function declaration like this:

```
int sum(int a, int b);
```

The a and b parameters are formal parameters.

We are calling the function like this:

```
int s = sum(10, 20); //Here 10 and 20 are actual parameters
```

or

```
int s = sum(n1, n2); //Here n1 and n2 are actual parameters
```

What is Function Call By Reference?

When we call a function by passing the addresses of actual parameters then this way of calling the function is known as call by reference. In call by reference, the operation performed on formal parameters, affects the value of actual parameters because all the operations performed on the value stored in the address of actual parameters. It may sound confusing first but the following example would clear your doubts.

Example of Function call by Reference

Lets take a simple example. Read the comments in the following program.

```
#include<stdio.h>
void increment(int*var)
{
/* Although we are performing the increment on variable
   * var, however the var is a pointer that holds the address
   * of variable num, which means the increment is actually done
   * on the address where value of num is stored.
   */
*var=*var+1;
}
int main()
{
int num=20;
/* This way of calling the function is known as call by
   * reference. Instead of passing the variable num, we are
   * passing the address of variable num
   */
   increment(&num);
   printf("Value of num is: %d", num);
return0;
}
```

Output

```
Value of num is:21
```

Example 2: Function Call by Reference – Swapping Numbers

Here we are swapping the numbers using call by reference. As you can see the values of the variables have been changed after calling the swapnum() function because the swap happened on the addresses of the variables num1 and num2.

```
#include
void swapnum (int*var1,int*var2 )
{
```

```
int tempnum ;
  tempnum =*var1 ;
*var1 =*var2 ;
*var2 = tempnum ;
}
int main()
{
int num1 =35, num2 =45;
  printf("Before swapping:");
  printf("\nnum1 value is %d", num1);
  printf("\nnum2 value is %d", num2);
/*calling swap function*/
  swapnum(&num1,&num2 );
  printf("\nAfter swapping:");
  printf("\nnum1 value is %d", num1);
  printf("\nnum2 value is %d", num2);
return0;
}
```

Output

```
Before swapping:
num1 value is35
num2 value is45
After swapping:
num1 value is45
num2 value is35
```

Passing Array to Function Using Call by Value Method

As we already know in this type of function call, the actual parameter is copied to the formal parameters.

```
#include<stdio.h>
void disp(char ch)
{
  printf("%c ", ch);
}
```

```
int main()
{
char arr[]={'a','b','c','d','e','f','g','h','i','j'};
for(int x=0; x<10; x++)
{
/* I'm passing each element one by one using subscript*/
    disp (arr[x]);
}
return0;
}
```

Output

```
a b c d e f g h i j
```

Passing Array to Function Using Call by Reference

When we pass the address of an array while calling a function then this is called function call by reference. When we pass an address as an argument, the function declaration should have a pointer as a parameter to receive the passed address.

```
#include<stdio.h>
void disp(int*num)
{
  printf("%d ",*num);
}
int main()
{
int arr[]={1,2,3,4,5,6,7,8,9,0};
for(int i=0; i<10; i++)
{
/* Passing addresses of array elements*/
     disp (&arr[i]);
}
return0;
}
```

Output

```
1234567890
```

How to Pass an Entire Array to a Function as an Argument?

In the above example, we have passed the address of each array element one by one using a for loop in C. However you can also pass an entire array to a function like this:

Note: The array name itself is the address of first element of that array. For example if array name is arr then you can say that **arr** is equivalent to the **&arr[0]**.

```
#include<stdio.h>
void myfuncn(int*var1,int var2)
{
  /* The pointer var1 is pointing to the first element of
   * the array and the var2 is the size of the array. In the
   * loop we are incrementing pointer so that it points to
   * the next element of the array on each increment.
   *
   */
for(int x=0; x<var2; x++)
{
     printf("Value of var_arr[%d] is: %d \n", x,*var1);
/*increment pointer for next element fetch*/
     var1++;
}
}
int main()
{
int var_arr[]={11,22,33,44,55,66,77};
   myfuncn(var_arr,7);
return0;
}
```

Output

```
Value of var_arr[0]is:11
Value of var_arr[1]is:22
Value of var_arr[2]is:33
Value of var_arr[3]is:44
Value of var_arr[4]is:55
Value of var_arr[5]is:66
Value of var_arr[6]is:77
```

7.4. Recursion Function

The process of calling a function by itself is called recursion and the function which calls itself is called recursive function. Recursion is used to solve various mathematical problems by dividing it into smaller problems. This method of solving a problem is called Divide and Conquer.

Syntax of Recursive Function

```
returntype recursive_func ([argument list])
{
  statements;
  ... ... ...
  recursive_func ([actual argument]);
  ... ... ...
}
```

Types of Recursion

- Direct Recursion.
- Indirect Recursion.

Direct Recursion

A function is said to be direct recursive if it calls itself directly.

Example 1: Program Function to Show Direct Recursion

```
int fibo (int n)
{
  if (n==1 || n==2)
    return 1;
  else
    return (fibo(n-1)+fibo(n-2));
}
```

In this program, *fibo()* is a direct recursive function. This is because, inside *fibo()* function, there is a statement which calls *fibo()* function again directly.

Indirect Recursion

A function is said to be indirect recursive if it calls another function and this new function calls the first calling function again.

Example 2 : C Program Function to Show Indirect Recursion

```
int func1(int n)
{
  if (n<=1)
    return 1;
  else
    return func2(n);
}

int func2(int n)
{
  return func1(n);
}
```

In this program, *func1()* calls *func2()*, which is a new function. But this new function *func2()* calls the first calling function, *func1()*, again. This makes the above function an indirect recursive function.

Example 3: C Program to Calculate Factorial of a Number Using Recursion

```
#include<stdio.h>
int factorial(int n)
{
  if(n==0)
    return 1;
  else
    return (factorial(n-1)*n);
}

int main()
{
  int num,f;
  printf("Enter a number: ");
  scanf("%d",&num);
  f=factorial(num);
  printf("Factorial of %d = %d",num,f);
  return 0;
```

```
}
```

Here, factorial is calculated using recursion. The formula for calculating factorial of a number n is,

n! = 1*2*...(n-1)*n

Again, we can see

(n-1)! = 1*2*...(n-1)

Hence we can write,

n! = (n-1)! * n

We have implemented this recursive relation in our program.

Here,

- The number whose factorial is to be found is stored in the variable *n.*
- A recursive function *factorial(num)* calculates the factorial of the number.
- As factorial is *(n-1)! * n, factorial* function calculates the factorial by recursively multiplying *n* with factorial of *(n-1).*
- Finally, when *n = 0,* it returns 1 because *0! = 1.*

Output

```
Enter a number: 7
Factorial of 7 = 5040
```

Example 4: C Program Print First n Fibonacci Numbers Using Recursion

```
#include<stdio.h>
int fibo(int num)
{
  if(num==1||num==2)
    return 1;
  else
    return (fibo(num-1)+fibo(num-2));  // recursive call
}
int main()
{
  int i,n;
```

```
    printf("Enter the required term: ");
    scanf("%d",&n);
    printf("First %d fibonacci numbers are\n",n);
    for (i=1; i<=n; i++)
      printf("%d\n",fibo(i));
    return 0;
}
```

This program uses recursion to generate Fibonacci series. In a Fibonacci series, n^{th} term can be obtained by adding $(n-1)^{th}$ and $(n-2)^{th}$ term. Mathematically,

tn = tn-1 + tn-2

Here,

- The number of fibonacci terms to be generated is taken from the user and stored in variable *n.*
- A for loop is used to loop through the number to be generated which is sent to the function *fibo*. This function is used to calculate and return fibonacci series.
- Inside *fibo*, if the term-number is 1 or 2, it returns 1. This is because, the first two terms of fibonacci series are both 1. The printed values are *1,1*.
- Then the next term-number *3* is passed onto *fibo* function, since it's not 1 or 2, the next term in the series is calculated by taking *fibo(n - 1) + fibo(n - 2)*, where *n = 3*. This calculates the last two terms in the fibonacci series. This is equivalent to *fibo(2) + fibo(1)*, which results in *1 + 1 = 2*.
- This recursive loop goes on finally printing the series as 1, 1, 2, 3, 5...

Output

```
Enter the required term: 7
First 7 fibonacci numbers are
1
1
2
3
5
8
13
```

Disadvantages of Recursion

- Recursive programs are generally slower than non recursive programs because it needs to make a function call so the program must save all its current state and retrieve them again later. This consumes more time making recursive programs slower.
- Recursive programs requires more memory to hold intermediate states in a stack. Non recursive programs don't have any intermediate states, hence they don't require any extra memory.

7.5. Exercises

1) What will be the output of the C program?

```
#include<stdio.h>
int main()
{
        function();
        return 0;
}
void function()
{
        printf("Function in C is awesome");
}
```

A. Function in C is awesome

B. no output

C. Runtime error

D. Compilation error

Output

Option: D

Explanation

Yes its a Compilation error, when compiler reads function(); it don't knew whether function() is available or not. So we have to initialize the function before main function.

2) What will be the output of the C program?

```
#include<stdio.h>
int main()
{
        main();
        return 0;
}
```

A. Runtime error

B. Compilation error

C. 0

D. none of the above

Output

Option: A

Explanation

Yes its a runtime error, here the main() function repeatedly called the main() and the program never ends.

3) What will be the output of the C program?

```
#include<stdio.h>
int function();
main()
{
        int i;
        i = function();
        printf("%d", i);
        return 0;
}
function()
{
        int a;
        a = 250;
        return 0;
}
```

A. Runtime error

B. 0

C. 250

D. No output

Output

Option: B

Explanation

Even though we declared a variable a = 250, we finally ask the compiler to return 0. Thus outputted 0.

4) What will be the output of the C program?

```
#include<stdio.h>
int function();
main()
{
		int i;
		i = function();
		printf("%d", i);
		return 0;
}
function()
{
		int a;
		a = 250;
}
```

A. 250

B. 0

C. 1

D. Some Garbage value

Output

Option: C

Explanation

Here function executed successfully and we don't return anything, by default C compiler returns 1 for its successful execution.

5) What will be the output of the C program?

```
#include<stdio.h>
int function(int, int);
int main()
{
		int a = 25, b = 24 + 1, c;
		printf("%d", function(a, b));
		return 0;
}
int function(int x, int y)
{
```

```
        return (x - (x == y));
}
```

A. Compilation error

B. 25

C. 1

D. 24

Output

Option: D

Explanation

Here function() returns 24.

return (25 - (25 == 25));

return (25 - 1);

return 24;

6) What will be the output of the C program?

```
#include<stdio.h>
int main()
{
        int num = _a_123(4);
        printf("%d\n", --num);
        return 0;
}
int _a_123(int num)
{
        return(num++);
}
```

A. 3

B. Compilation error

C. 4

D. 5

Output

Option: A

Explanation

In this program _a_123(4) is a valid function and it passes 4 as a value type. In function _a_123(int num) we just return that number with post increment which means the function simply returns 4 Then in printf we display the value stored in the variable num with predecrement. Thus it outputted 3.

7) What will be the output of the C program by considering 'c' as a User input?

```
#include<stdio.h>
int main()
{
        char c = ' ', x;
        getc(c);
        if((c >= 'a') && (c <= 'z'))
        x = convert(c);
        printf("%c", x);
        return 0;
}
```

A. Runtime Error

B. Any symbols or special characters

C. Compilation Error

D. B

Output

Option: C

Explanation

getc() can only be used in file handling and not to get a character

8) What will be the output of the C program?

```
#include<stdio.h>
int main()
{
        int num = returns(sizeof(float));
        printf("Value is %d", ++num);
        return 0;
}
int returns(int returns)
```

```
{
        returns += 5.01;
        return(returns);
}
```

A. 9

B. Compilation error

C. 10

D. None of the above

Output

Option: C

Explanation

Here, returns () is a valid function, which passes 8 as a value type. Inside returns function we encounter

returns += 5.01;

i.e) returns = returns + 5.01;

returns = 4 + 5.01;

returns = 9;

Thus the function returns 9;

In printf it outputted the num variable with pre increment thus outputted 10.

9) What will be the output of the C program?

```
#include<stdio.h>
int recursive(int i)
{
        static int count = 0;
        count = count + i;
        return count;
}
int main()
{
        int i, j;
        for (i = 0; i <= 5; i++)
        j = recursive(i);
        printf("%d\n", j);
        return 0;
}
```

A. 5

B. Compilation error

C. 15

D. 0

Output

Option: C

Explanation

static int count = 0 is only for the first time od iteration because its static.

Iteration 1

count = count + i;

count = 0 + 0;

count = 0;

Iteration 2

count = count + 1;

count = 0 + 1;

count = 0;

Iteration 3

count = count + 2;

count = 1 + 2;

count = 3;

Iteration 4

count = count + 3;

count = 3 + 3;

count = 6;

Iteration 5

count = count + 4;

count = 6 + 4;

count = 10;

Iteration 6

count = count + 5;

count = 10 + 5;

count = 15;

10) What will be the output of the C program?

```
#include<stdio.h>
int num = 5;
int main()
{
        fun();
        fun();
        return 0;
}
int fun()
{
        static int num = 2;
        printf("%d ",num);
        num++;
        return 0;
}
```

A. 2 3

B. 2 2

C. 5 5

D. 5 6

Output

Option: A

Explanation

int num = 2 is static and it executes only for the first time of function execution. Thus outputted 2 3.

Try by Yourself

1) What will be the output of the C program?

```
#include<stdio.h>
void fun(int);
```

```
int main()
{
        int a = 3;
        fun(a);
        return 0;
}
void fun(int n)
{
        if (n > 0)
        {
                fun(--n);
                printf("%d ", n);
        }
}
```

A. 1 2 3

B. No Output

C. 0 1 2

D. 0

2) What will be the output of the C program?

```
#include<stdio.h>
int main()
{
        int i;
        i = main();
        printf("%d", i);
int main()
{
        int a;
        a = 5 * 5;
        return a;
}
return 0;
}
```

A. Compilation error

B. Runtime error

C. address

D. 25

3) What is the output of this C code?

```
int main()
{
void foo(), f();
f();
}
void foo()
{
printf("2 ");
}
void f()
{
printf("1 ");
foo();
}
```

A. Compile time error as foo is local to main

B. 1 2

C. 2 1

D. Compile time error due to declaration of functions inside main

4) What is the output of this C code?

```
int main()
{
void foo();
void f()
{
foo();
}
f();
}
void foo()
{
printf("2 ");
}
```

A. 2 2

B. 2

C. Compile time error

D. Depends on the compiler

5) What is the output of this C code?

```
void main()
{
    static int x = 3;
    x++;
    if (x <= 5)
    {
        printf("hi");
        main();
    }
}
```

A. Run time error

B. hi

C. infinite hi

D. hi hi

6) What will happen after compiling and running following code?

```
main()
{
    printf("%p", main);
}
```

A. Error

B. Will make an infinite loop.

C. Some address will be printed.

D. None of these.

7) Determine output:

```
main()
{
    int i = abc(10);
    printf("%d", --i);
```

```
}
int abc(int i)
{
    return(i++);
}
```

A.10

B.9

C.11

D. None of these

8) What will be the output of the following program code?

```
main()
{
    static int var = 5;
    printf("%d ", var--);
    if(var)
        main();
}
```

A. 5 5 5 5 5

B. 5 4 3 2 1

C. Infinite Loop

D. Compilation Error

9) What will be printed when this program is executed?

```
int f(int x)
{
  if(x <= 4)
    return x;
  return f(--x);
}
void main()
{
  printf("%d ", f(7));
}
```

A.4567

B.1234

C.4

D. Syntax Error

10) What will be the output of the program?

```
#include<stdio.h>
int i;
int fun();
int main()
{
while(i)
  {
    fun();
    main();
  }
  printf("Hello\n");
return0;
}
int fun()
{
  printf("Hi");
}
```

A. Hello

B. Hi Hello

C. No Output

D. Infinite Loop

Answer

1)c 2)b 3)b 4)d 5)d 6)c 7)b 8)b 9)c 10)a

Storage Class in C

Storage class in C decides the part of storage to allocate memory for a variable, it also determines the scope of a variable.

All variables defined in a C program get some physical location in memory where variable's value is stored. Memory and CPU registers are types of memory locations where a variable's value can be stored. The storage class of a variable in C determines the life time of the variable if this is 'global' or 'local'.

Along with the life time of a variable, storage class also determines variable's storage location (memory or registers), the scope (visibility level) of the variable, and the initial value of the variable. There are four storage classes in C those are *automatic, register, static,* and *external*. The following storage classes are most oftenly used in C programming.

1. Automatic variables.
2. External variables.
3. Static variables.
4. Register variables.

Automatic Variables: Auto

Scope: Variable defined with auto storage class are local to the function block inside which they are defined.

Default Initial Value: Any random value i.e garbage value.

Lifetime: Till the end of the function/method block where the variable is defined.

A variable declared inside a function without any storage class specification, is by default an **automatic variable.**

They are created when a function is called and are destroyed **automatically** when the function's execution is completed.

Automatic variables can also be called **local variables** because they are local to a function. By default they are assigned **garbage value** by the compiler.

```
#include<stdio.h>
void main()
{
  int detail;
//or
  auto int details;//Both are same
}
```

External or Global Variable

Scope: Global i.e everywhere in the program.

These variables are not bound by any function, they are available everywhere.

Default initial value: 0(zero).

Lifetime: Till the program doesn't finish its execution, you can access global variables.

A variable that is declared outside any function is a **Global Variable**. Global variables remain available throughout the program execution. By default, initial value of the Global variable is 0(zero).

One important thing to remember about global variable is that their values can be changed by any function in the program.

```
#include<stdio.h>
int number;// global variable
void main()
{
number =10;
printf("I am in main function. My value is %d\n", number);
fun1();//function calling, discussed in next topic
fun2();//function calling, discussed in next topic
}
/* This is function 1 */
fun1()
{
number =20;
printf("I am in function fun1. My value is %d", number);
}
/* This is function 1 */
fun2()
{
printf("\nI am in function fun2. My value is %d", number);
}
```

```
I am in function main. My value is 10
I am in function fun1. My value is 20
I am in function fun2. My value is 20
```

Here the global variable number is available to all three functions and thus, if one function changes the value of the variable, it gets changed in every function.

Note: Declaring the storage class as global or external for all the variables in a program can waste a lot of memory space because these variables have a lifetime till the end of the program.

Thus, variables, which are not needed till the end of the program, will still occupy the memory and thus, memory will be wasted.

Extern Keyword

The extern keyword is used with a variable to inform the compiler that this variable is declared somewhere else. The extern declaration does not allocate storage for variables.

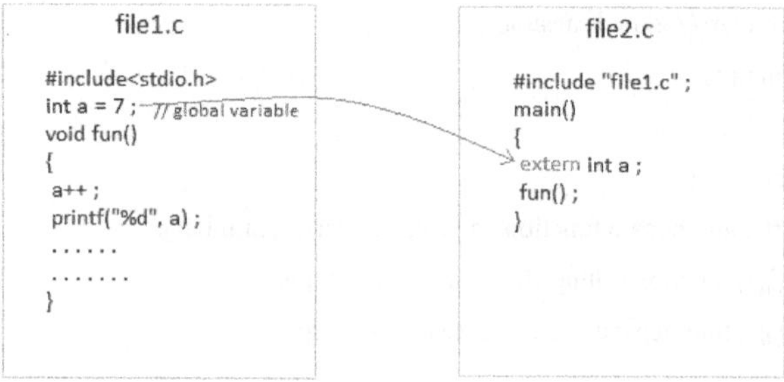

global variable from one file can be used in other using extern keyword.

Problem when extern is not used

```
int main()
{
  a =10;//Error: cannot find definition of variable 'a'
printf("%d", a);
}
```

Example using extern in same file

```
int main()
{
  extern int x;//informs the compiler that it is defined somewhere else
  x =10;
printf("%d", x);
}
int x;//Global variable x
```

Static Variables

Scope: Local to the block in which the variable is defined

Default initial value: 0(Zero).

Lifetime: Till the whole program doesn't finish its execution.

A static variable tells the compiler to persist/save the variable until the end of program. Instead of creating and destroying a variable every time when it comes into and goes out of scope, staticvariable is initialized only once and remains into existence till the end of the program. A staticvariable can either be internal or external depending upon the place of declaration. Scope of **internal static** variable remains inside the function in which it is defined. **External static** variables remain restricted to scope of file in which they are declared.

They are assigned **0 (zero)** as default value by the compiler.

```
#include<stdio.h>
void test();//Function declaration (discussed in next topic)
int main()
{
test();
test();
test();
}
void test()
{
  static int a =0;//a static variable
  a = a +1;
printf("%d\t",a);
}
1 2 3
```

Register Variable

Scope: Local to the function in which it is declared.

Default initial value: Any random value i.e garbage value

Lifetime: Till the end of function/method block, in which the variable is defined.

Register variables inform the compiler to store the variable in CPU register instead of memory.

Register variables have faster accessibility than a normal variable. Generally, the frequently used variables are kept in registers. But only a few variables can be placed inside registers. One application of register storage class can be in using loops, where the variable gets used a number of times in the program, in a very short span of time.

NOTE: We can never get the address of such variables.

Syntax

register int number;

Note: Even though we have declared the storage class of our variable number as register, we cannot surely say that the value of the variable would be stored in a register. This is because the number of registers in a CPU are limited. Also, CPU registers are meant to do a lot of important work. Thus, sometimes they may not be free. In such scenario, the variable works as if its storage class is auto.

Which Storage Class Should be Used and When

To improve the speed of execution of the program and to carefully use the memory space occupied by the variables, following points should be kept in mind while using storage classes:

- We should use static storage class only when we want the value of the variable to remain same every time we call it using different function calls.
- We should use register storage class only for those variables that are used in our program very oftenly. CPU registers are limited and thus should be used carefully.
- We should use external or global storage class only for those variables that are being used by almost all the functions in the program.
- If we do not have the purpose of any of the above mentioned storage classes, then we should use the automatic storage class.

CHAPTER 8

STRINGS IN C

8.1. Introduction

Strings are actually one-dimensional array of characters terminated by a **null** character '\0'. Thus a null-terminated string contains the characters that comprise the string followed by a **null**.

The following declaration and initialization create a string consisting of the word "Hello". To hold the null character at the end of the array, the size of the character array containing the string is one more than the number of characters in the word "Hello."

```
char greeting[6] = {'H', 'e', 'l', 'l', 'o', '\0'};
```

If you follow the rule of array initialization then you can write the above statement as follows.

```
char greeting[] = "Hello";
```

Let us now look at a sample program to get a clear understanding of declaring and initializing a string in C and also how to print a string.

```
// C program to illustrate strings
#include<stdio.h>
int main()
{
  // declare and initialize string
  char str[] = "Welcome";
     // print string
  printf("%s",str);
     return 0;
  }
```

Output

Welcome.

We can see in the above program that strings can be printed using a normal printf statements just like we print any other variable. Unlike arrays we do not need to print a string, character by character. The C language does not provide an inbuilt data type for strings but it has an access specifier "**%s**" which can be used to directly print and read strings.

Below is a Sample Program to Read a String from User

```
// C program to read strings
#include<stdio.h>
int main()
{
  // declaring string
  char str[50];
     // reading string
  scanf("%s",str);
     // print string
  printf("%s",str);
   return 0;
}
```

You can see in the above program that string can also be read using a single scanf statement. Also you might be thinking that why we have not used the '&' sign with string name 'str' in scanf statement! To understand this you will have to recall your knowledge of scanf. We know that the '&' sign is used to provide the address of the variable to the scanf() function to store the value read in memory. As str[] is a character array so using str without braces '[' and ']' will give the base address of this string. That's why we have not used '&' in this case as we are already providing the base address of the string to scanf.

8.2. Passing Function

Passing strings to function: As strings are character arrays, so we can pass strings to function in a same way we pass an array to a function. Below is a sample program to do this:

```
// C program to illustrate how to
// pass string to functions
#include<stdio.h>
 void printStr(char str[])
{
  printf("String is : %s",str);
}
int main()
```

```
{
  // declare and initialize string
  char str[] = "Welcome";
     // print string by passing string
  // to a different function
  printStr(str);
     return 0;
  }
```

Run on IDE

Output

String is: Welcome

8.3. C String Functions

- String.h header file supports all the string functions in C language. All the string functions are given below.
- Click on each string function name below for detail description and example programs.

String functions	Description
strcat ( )	Concatenates str2 at the end of str1
strncat ( )	Appends a portion of string to another
strcpy ( )	Copies str2 into str1
strncpy ( )	Copies given number of characters of one string to another
strlen ( )	Gives the length of str1
strcmp ( )	Returns 0 if str1 is same as str2. Returns <0 if strl < str2. Returns >0 if str1 > str2
strcmpi ( )	Same as strcmp() function. But, this function negotiates case. "A" and "a" are treated as same.
strchr ( )	Returns pointer to first occurrence of char in str1
strrchr ( )	last occurrence of given character in a string is found
strstr ( )	Returns pointer to first occurrence of str2 in str1
strrstr ( )	Returns pointer to last occurrence of str2 in str1
strdup ( )	Duplicates the string
strlwr ( )	Converts string to lowercase
strupr ( )	Converts string to uppercase
strrev ( )	Reverses the given string
strset ( )	Sets all character in a string to given character
strnset ( )	It sets the portion of characters in a string to given character
strtok ( )	Tokenizing given string using delimiter

C String Function – Strlen

Syntax

size_t strlen(constchar*str)

size_t represents unsigned short

It returns the length of the string without including end character **(terminating char '\0')**.

Example of strlen

```
#include<stdio.h>
#include<string.h>
int main()
{
char str1[20]="BeginnersBook";
   printf("Length of string str1: %d", strlen(str1));
return0;
}
Output:
Length of string str1:13
```

strlen vs Size

strlen returns you the length of the string stored in array, however sizeof returns the total allocated size assigned to the array. So if I consider the above example again then the following statements would return the below values.

strlen(str1) returned value 13.

sizeof(str1) would return value 20 as the array size is 20 (see the first statement in main function).

C String Function – Strnlen

Syntax

```
size_t strnlen(constchar*str,size_t maxlen)
```

size_t represents unsigned short

It returns length of the string if it is less than the value specified for maxlen (maximum length) otherwise it returns maxlen value.

Example of Strnlen

```
#include<stdio.h>
#include<string.h>
int main()
{
char str1[20]="BeginnersBook";
   printf("Length of string str1 when maxlen is 30: %d", strnlen(str1,30));
```

```
    printf("Length of string str1 when maxlen is 10: %d", strnlen(str1,10));
return0;
}
```

Output

```
Length of string str1 when maxlen is 30: 13
Length of string str1 when maxlen is 10: 10
```

Have you noticed the output of second printf statement, even though the string length was 13 it returned only 10 because the maxlen was 10.

C String Function – Strcmp

```
int strcmp(constchar*str1,constchar*str2)
```

It compares the two strings and returns an integer value. If both the strings are same (equal) then this function would return 0 otherwise it may return a negative or positive value based on the comparison.

If string1 < string2 OR string1 is a substring of string2 then it would result in a negative value. If string1 > string2 then it would return positive value.

If string1 == string2 then you would get 0(zero) when you use this function for compare strings.

Example of Strcmp

```
#include<stdio.h>
#include<string.h>
int main()
{
char s1[20]="BeginnersBook";
char s2[20]="BeginnersBook.COM";
if(strcmp(s1, s2)==0)
{
    printf("string 1 and string 2 are equal");
}else
{
    printf("string 1 and 2 are different");
}
return0;
}
```

Output

```
string1and2 are different
```

C String Function – Strncmp

int strncmp(constchar*str1,constchar*str2,size_t n)

size_t is for unassigned short

It compares both the string till n characters or in other words it compares first n characters of both the strings.

Example of Strncmp

```
#include<stdio.h>
#include<string.h>
int main()
{
char s1[20]="BeginnersBook";
char s2[20]="BeginnersBook.COM";
/* below it is comparing first 8 characters of s1 and s2*/
if(strncmp(s1, s2,8)==0)
{
    printf("string 1 and string 2 are equal");
}else
{
    printf("string 1 and 2 are different");
}
return0;
}
```

Output

string1 andstring2 are equal

C String function – strcat

char*strcat(char*str1,char*str2)

It concatenates two strings and returns the concatenated string.

Example of Strcat

```
#include<stdio.h>
#include<string.h>
int main()
{
```

```
char s1[10]="Hello";
char s2[10]="World";
   strcat(s1,s2);
   printf("Output string after concatenation: %s", s1);
return0;
}
```

Output

```
Outputstring after concatenation:HelloWorld
```

C String function – strncat

char*strncat(char*str1,char*str2,int n)

It concatenates n characters of str2 to string str1. A terminator char ('\0') will always be appended at the end of the concatenated string.

Example of Strncat

```
#include<stdio.h>
#include<string.h>
int main()
{
char s1[10]="Hello";
char s2[10]="World";
   strncat(s1,s2,3);
   printf("Concatenation using strncat: %s", s1);
return0;
}
```

Output

```
Concatenationusing strncat:HelloWor
```

C String function – strcpy

char*strcpy(char*str1,char*str2)

It copies the string str2 into string str1, including the end character (terminator char '\0').

Example of Strcpy

```
#include<stdio.h>
#include<string.h>
int main()
```

```
{
char s1[30]="string 1";
char s2[30]="string 2 : I'm gonna copied into s1";
/* this function has copied s2 into s1*/
   strcpy(s1,s2);
   printf("String s1 is: %s", s1);
return0;
}
```

Output

```
String s1 is:string2: I'm gonna copied into s1
```

C String Function – Strncpy

```
char *strncpy( char *str1, char *str2, size_t n)
```

size_t is unassigned short and n is a number.

Case1: If length of str2 > n then it just copies first n characters of str2 into str1.

Case2: If length of str2 < n then it copies all the characters of str2 into str1 and appends several terminator chars('\0') to accumulate the length of str1 to make it n.

Example of Strncpy

```
#include<stdio.h>
#include<string.h>
int main()
{
char first[30]="string 1";
char second[30]="string 2: I'm using strncpy now";
/* this function has copied first 10 chars of s2 into s1*/
   strncpy(s1,s2,12);
   printf("String s1 is: %s", s1);
return0;
}
```

Output

```
String s1 is:string2: I'm
```

C String Function – Strchr

char*strchr(char*str,int ch)

It searches string str for character ch (you may be wondering that in above definition I have given data type of ch as int, don't worry I didn't make any mistake it should be int only. The thing is when we give any character while using strchr then it internally gets converted into integer for better searching.

Example of Strchr

```
#include<stdio.h>
#include<string.h>
int main()
{
char mystr[30]="I'm an example of function strchr";
   printf ("%s", strchr(mystr,'f'));
return0;
}
```

Output

```
f function strchr
```

C String Function – STRRCHR

char*strrchr(char*str,int ch)

It is similar to the function strchr, the only difference is that it searches the string in reverse order, now you would have understood why we have extra r in strrchr, yes you guessed it correct, it is for reverse only.

Now let's take the same above example:

```
#include<stdio.h>
#include<string.h>
int main()
{
char mystr[30]="I'm an example of function strchr";
   printf ("%s", strrchr(mystr,'f'));
return0;
}
```

Output

```
function strchr
```

Why output is different than strchr? It is because it started searching from the end of the string and found the first 'f' in function instead of 'of'.

C String function – strstr

char*strstr(char*str,char*srch_term)

It is similar to strchr, except that it searches for string srch_term instead of a single char.

Example of Strstr

```
#include<stdio.h>
#include<string.h>
int main()
{
char inputstr[70]="String Function in C at welcome";
   printf ("Output string is: %s", strstr(inputstr,'Begi'));
return0;
}
```

Output

```
Outputstringis:welcome
```

You can also use this function in place of strchr as you are allowed to give single char also in place of search_term string.

C Program to Reverse Words in a Line

```
#include<stdio.h>
#include<string.h>
int string_length(char s[]){
int i=0;
while(s[i]!='\0')
   i++;
return i;
}
void string_reverse(char st[]){
int i,j,len;
char ch;
```

```
  j = len = string_length(st)-1;
  i =0;
while(i < j){
    ch = st[j];
    st[j]= st[i];
    st[i]= ch;
    i++;
    j--;
}
}
int main (void){
char line[]="Taj Mahal is one of the seven wonders of the world";
char reverse[100]="",temp[50];
int i,j,n;
  n = string_length(line);
for(i =0; i < n; i++){
for(j =0; i < n && line[i]!=' ';++i,++j){
      temp[j]= line[i];
}
    temp[j]='\0';
    string_reverse(temp);
    strcat(reverse, temp);
    strcat(reverse," ");
}
  printf("Original - %s\n", line);
  printf("Reversed - %s\n",reverse);
return0;
}
```

Output

Output of this program should be:

```
Original - Taj Mahal is one of the seven wonders of the world
Reversed - jaT lahaM si eno fo eht neves srednow fo eht dlrow
```

C Program to Reverse a Line

```
#include<stdio.h>
#include<string.h>
int string_length(char s[]){
int i=0;
while(s[i]!='\0')
    i++;
return i;
}
void string_reverse(char st[]){
int i,j,len;
char ch;
  j = len = string_length(st)-1;
  i =0;
while(i < j){
    ch = st[j];
    st[j]= st[i];
    st[i]= ch;
    i++;
    j--;
}
}
int main (void){
char line[]="Taj Mahal is one of the seven wonders of the world";
char reverse[100]="", temp[50];
int i, j, n;
  n = string_length(line);
for(i = n-1; i >=0;--i){
for(j =0; i >=0&& line[i]!=' ';--i,++j)
      temp[j]= line[i];
    temp[j]='\0';
    string_reverse(temp);
    strcat(reverse,temp);
    strcat(reverse," ");
```

```
}
  printf("Original - %s\n", line);
  printf("Reversed - %s\n",reverse);
return0;
}
```

Output

Output of this program should be,

Original - Taj Mahal is one of the seven wonders of the world.

Reversed - world the of wonders seven the of one is Mahal Taj

8.4. Exercises

1) What will be the output of following program ?

```
#include <stdio.h>
#include <string.h>
int main()
{
  int val=0;
  char str[]="google.Com";

  val=strcmp(str,"google.com");
  printf("%d",val);
  return 0;
}
```

A. 0

B. 1

C. -1

D. Error

Output

Option c

Explanation

Strings are not equal, hence strcmp will return -1.

2) What will be the output of following program?

```
#include <stdio.h>
#include <string.h>
 int main()
{
   char str[];
   strcpy(str,"Hello");
   printf("%s",str);
   return 0;
}
```

A. Hello

B. Error

C. No Output

D. Null

Output

Explanation

Option b

'str' Unknown Size

At the time of str declaration, size is empty, it may be possible when you are initializing string with declaration (like char str[]="Hello";

3) What will be the output of the program ?

```
#include<stdio.h>
#include<string.h>
int main()
{
char str1[20] = "Hello", str2[20] = " World";
   printf("%s\n", strcpy(str2, strcat(str1, str2)));
return0;
}
```

A.Hello

B.World

C.Hello World

D.World Hello

Output

Option C

Explanation

Step 1: char str1[20] = "Hello", str2[20] = " World"; The variable str1 and str2 is declared as an array of characters and initialized with value "Hello" and " World" respectively.

Step 2: printf("%s\n", strcpy(str2, strcat(str1, str2)));

=> strcat(str1, str2)) it append the string str2 to str1. The result will be stored in str1.

Therefore str1contains "Hello World".

=> strcpy(str2, "Hello World") it copies the "Hello World" to the variable str2.

Hence it prints "Hello World".

4) What will be the output of the program?

```
#include<stdio.h>
int main()
{
  char p[] = "%d\n";
  p[1] = 'c';
  printf(p, 65);
  return 0;
}
```

A. A

B. A

C. C

D. 65

Answer

Option A

Explanation

Step 1: char p[] = "%d\n"; The variable p is declared as an array of characters and initialized with string "%d".

Step 2: p[1] = 'c'; Here, we overwrite the second element of array p by 'c'. So array p becomes "%c".

Step 3: printf(p, 65); becomes printf("%c", 65);

Therefore it prints the ASCII value of 65. The output is 'A'.

5) What will be the output of the program?

```
#include<stdio.h>
#include<string.h>
int main()
{
   printf("%d\n", strlen("123456"));
   return 0;
}
```

A.6

B.12

C.7

D.2

Answer

Option A

Explanation

The function strlen returns the number of characters in the given string.

Therefore, strlen("123456") returns 6.

Hence the output of the program is "6".

6) What will be the output of the program?

```
#include<stdio.h>
int main()
{
   printf(5+"Good Morning\n");
   return 0;
}
```

A. Good Morning

B. Good

C. M

D. Morning

Answer

Option D

Explanation

printf(5+"Good Morning\n"); It skips the 5 characters and prints the given string.

Hence the output is "Morning"

7) What will be the output of the program If characters 'a', 'b' and 'c' enter are supplied as input?

```
#include<stdio.h>
int main()
{
  void fun();
  fun();
  printf("\n");
  return 0;
}
void fun()
{
  char c;
  if((c = getchar())!= '\n')
    fun();
  printf("%c", c);
}
```

A. abc abc

B. bca

C. Infinite loop

D. Cba

Answer

Option D

Explanation

Step 1: void fun(); This is the prototype for the function fun().

Step 2: fun(); The function fun() is called here.

The function fun() gets a character input and the input is terminated by an enter key(New line character). It prints the given character in the reverse order.

The given input characters are "abc"

Output

cba

8) What will be the output of the program ?

```
#include<stdio.h>
int main()
{
  printf("%d, %d, %d", sizeof(3.0f), sizeof('3'), sizeof(3.0));
  return 0;
}
```

A.8, 1, 4

B.4, 4, 8

C.4, 2, 4

D.10, 3, 4

Answer

Option B

Explanation

Step 1

printf("%d, %d, %d", sizeof(3.0f), sizeof('3'), sizeof(3.0));

The sizeof function returns the size of the given expression.

sizeof(3.0f) is a floating point constant. The size of float is 4 bytes

sizeof('3') It converts '3' in to ASCII value.. The size of int is 2 bytes

sizeof(3.0) is a double constant. The size of double is 8 bytes

Hence the output of the program is 4,2,8

Note: The above program may produce different output in other platform due to the platform dependency of C compiler.

In Turbo C, 4 2 8. But in GCC, the output will be 4 4 8.

9) What will be the output of the program?

```
#include<stdio.h>
int main()
{
  int i;
  char a[] = "\0";
  if(printf("%s", a))
    printf("The string is empty\n");
  else
    printf("The string is not empty\n");
```

```
    return 0;
}
```

A.The string is empty

B.The string is not empty

C.No output

D.0

Answer

Option B

Explanation

The function printf() returns the number of charecters printed on the console.

Step 1: char a[] = "\0"; The variable a is declared as an array of characters and it initialized with "\0". It denotes that the string is empty.

Step 2: if(printf("%s", a)) The printf() statement does not print anything, so it returns '0'(zero). Hence the if condition is failed.

In the else part it prints "The string is not empty".

10) What will be the output of the program?

```
#include<stdio.h>
int main()
{
    char str[] = "Nagpur";
    str[0]='K';
    printf("%s, ", str);
    str = "Kanpur";
    printf("%s", str+1);
    return 0;
}
```

A. Kagpur, Kanpur

B. Nagpur, Kanpur

C. Kagpur, anpur

D. Error

Answer

Option D

Explanation

The statement str = "Kanpur"; generates the LVALUE required error. We have to use strcpy function to copy a string.

To remove error we have to change this statement str = "Kanpur"; to strcpy(str, "Kanpur");

The program prints the string "anpur"

Try by Yourself

1) What is the output of this C code?

```
#include <stdio.h>
int main()
{
char*str ="hello, world";
char*str1 ="hello, world";
if(strcmp(str, str1))
printf("equal");
else
printf("unequal");
}
```

a) equal

b) unequal

c) Compilation error

d) Depends on the compiler

2) What is the output of this C code?

```
#include <stdio.h>
int main()
{
char*str ="hello, world";
char*str1 ="hello, world";
if(strcmp(str, str1))
printf("equal");
else
printf("unequal");
}
```

a) equal

b) unequal

c) Compilation error

d) Depends on the compiler

3) What will be the output of the program?

```
#include<stdio.h>
int main()
{
   char str1[] = "Hello";
   char str2[] = "Hello";
   if(str1 == str2)
      printf("Equal\n");
   else
      printf("Unequal\n");
   return 0;
}
```

A. Equal

B. Unequal

C. Error

D. None of above

4) What will be the output of the program?

```
#include<stdio.h>
#include<string.h>
int main()
{
   printf("%c\n", "abcdefgh"[4]);
   return 0;
}
```

a). Error

b). D

c). E

d). Abcdefgh

Answer

1)b 2)c 3)b 4)c

CHAPTER 9

POINTERS IN C

9.1. Introduction

Pointers in C are easy and fun to learn. Some C programming tasks are performed more easily with pointers, and other tasks, such as dynamic memory allocation, cannot be performed without using pointers. So it becomes necessary to learn pointers to become a perfect C programmer. Let's start learning them in simple and easy steps.

As you know, every variable is a memory location and every memory location has its address defined which can be accessed using ampersand (&) operator, which denotes an address in memory. Consider the following example, which prints the address of the variables defined.

```
#include<stdio.h>
int main (){
int var1;
char var2[10];
  printf("Address of var1 variable: %x\n",&var1 );
  printf("Address of var2 variable: %x\n",&var2 );
return0;
}
```

When the above code is compiled and executed, it produces the following result –

```
Address of var1 variable: bff5a400
Address of var2 variable: bff5a3f6
```

What are Pointers?

A **pointer** is a variable whose value is the address of another variable, i.e., direct address of the memory location. Like any variable or constant, you must declare a pointer before using it to store any variable address. The general form of a pointer variable declaration is –

```
type *var-name;
```

Here, **type** is the pointer's base type; it must be a valid C data type and **var-name** is the name of the pointer variable. The asterisk * used to declare a pointer is the same asterisk used for multiplication. However, in this statement the asterisk is being used to designate a variable as a pointer. Take a look at some of the valid pointer declarations –

```
int   *ip;   /* pointer to an integer */
double *dp;   /* pointer to a double */
float *fp;   /* pointer to a float */
char  *ch    /* pointer to a character */
```

The actual data type of the value of all pointers, whether integer, float, character, or otherwise, is the same, a long hexadecimal number that represents a memory address. The only difference between pointers of different data types is the data type of the variable or constant that the pointer points to.

How to Use Pointers?

There are a few important operations, which we will do with the help of pointers very frequently. (a) We define a pointer variable, (b) assign the address of a variable to a pointer and (c) finally access the value at the address available in the pointer variable. This is done by using unary operator ***** that returns the value of the variable located at the address specified by its operand. The following example makes use of these operations.

```
#include<stdio.h>
int main (){
intvar=20;/* actual variable declaration */
int*ip;/* pointer variable declaration */
  ip =&var;/* store address of var in pointer variable*/
  printf("Address of var variable: %x\n",&var);
/* address stored in pointer variable */
  printf("Address stored in ip variable: %x\n", ip );
/* access the value using the pointer */
  printf("Value of *ip variable: %d\n",*ip );
return0;
}
```

When the above code is compiled and executed, it produces the following result.

```
Address of var variable: bffd8b3c
Address stored in ip variable: bffd8b3c
Value of *ip variable: 20
```

9.2. C Pointers – Operators that are Used with Pointers

Lets discuss the operators & and * that are used with Pointers in C.

"Address of"(&) Operator

We have already seen in the first example that we can display the address of a variable using ampersand sign. I have used &num to access the address of variable num. The **& operator** is also known as "**Address of**" Operator.

```
printf("Address of var is: %p", &num);
```

Point to note: %p is a format specifier which is used for displaying the address in hex format.

Now that you know how to get the address of a variable but **how to store that address in some other variable?** That's where pointers comes into picture. As mentioned in the beginning of this guide, pointers in C programming are used for holding the address of another variables.

Pointer is just like another variable, the main difference is that it stores address of another variable rather than a value.

"Value at Address"(*) Operator

The * Operator is also known as **Value at address** operator.

How to Declare a Pointer?

```
int*p1 /*Pointer to an integer variable*/

double*p2 /*Pointer to a variable of data type double*/

char*p3 /*Pointer to a character variable*/

float*p4 /*pointer to a float variable*/
```

The above are the few examples of pointer declarations. **If you need a pointer to store the address of integer variable then the data type of the pointer should be int.** Same case is with the other data types.

By using * operator we can access the value of a variable through a pointer.

For example:

```
double a =10;
double*p;
p =&a;
```

*p would give us the value of the variable a. The following statement would display 10 as output.

```
printf("%d",*p);
```

Similarly if we assign a value to *pointer like this:

```
*p =200;
```

It would change the value of variable a. The statement above will change the value of a from 10 to 200.

*Example of Pointer demonstrating the use of & and **

```
#include<stdio.h>
int main()
{
/* Pointer of integer type, this can hold the
  * address of a integer type variable.
  */
int*p;
intvar=10;
/* Assigning the address of variable var to the pointer
  * p. The p can hold the address of var because var is
  * an integer type variable.
  */
  p=&var;
  printf("Value of variable var is: %d",var);
  printf("\nValue of variable var is: %d",*p);
  printf("\nAddress of variable var is: %p",&var);
  printf("\nAddress of variable var is: %p", p);
  printf("\nAddress of pointer p is: %p",&p);
return0;
}
```

Output

```
Value of variable varis:10
Value of variable varis:10
Address of variable varis:0x7fff5ed98c4c
Address of variable varis:0x7fff5ed98c4c
Address of pointer p is:0x7fff5ed98c50
```

9.3. NULL Pointer

It is always a good practice to assign a NULL value to a pointer variable in case you do not have an exact address to be assigned. This is done at the time of variable declaration. A pointer that is assigned NULL is called a **null**pointer.

The NULL pointer is a constant with a value of zero defined in several standard libraries. Consider the following program.

```
#include<stdio.h>
int main (){
int*ptr = NULL;
  printf("The value of ptr is : %x\n", ptr );
return0;
}
```

When the above code is compiled and executed, it produces the following result –

```
The value of ptr is 0
```

In most of the operating systems, programs are not permitted to access memory at address 0 because that memory is reserved by the operating system. However, the memory address 0 has special significance; it signals that the pointer is not intended to point to an accessible memory location. But by convention, if a pointer contains the null (zero) value, it is assumed to point to nothing.

To check for a null pointer, you can use an 'if' statement as follows.

```
if(ptr)   /* succeeds if p is not null */
if(!ptr)  /* succeeds if p is null */
```

Here are Some Features of Pointers

- By using pointers we can get multiple values from the function, as we know a function can return only one value but by passing arguments as pointers we can get more than one values from the pointer.
- By using pointers dynamic memory can be created according to the program use. We can save memory from static (compile time) declarations.
- By using pointers we can design and develop complex data structures like STACK, QUEUE, LINKED LIST etc.

- ***Amazing feature of pointes***: Pointers provide **direct memory access.**

Here are Some Disadvantages of the Pointers

Since pointers has many features but there are some disadvantages of pointers.

- Failed to protect memory addresses (locations) - Since pointer can access direct memory so memory cannot be protected.
- Uninitialized pointers can cause of segmentation fault.
- Pointers variables are slower than normal variables.
- Pointers always required Free Memory for Dynamically Allocated Memory.

An Example of C Pointers

Consider the following code.

Code

```
#include <stdio.h>
int main(void)
{
   char ch = 'c';
   char *chptr = &ch;
   int i = 20;
   int *intptr = &i;
   float f = 1.20000;
   float *fptr = &f;
   char *ptr = "I am a string";
   printf("\n [%c], [%d], [%f], [%c], [%s]\n", *chptr, *intptr, *fptr, *ptr, ptr);
   return 0;
}
```

Output

```
$ ./pointers
 [c], [20], [1.200000], [I], [I am a string]
```

To debug a C program, use gdb. The above code covers all the common pointers. The first three of them are very trivial now to understand so lets concentrate on the fourth one. In the fourth example, a character pointer points to a string.

In C, a string is nothing but an array of characters. So we have no staring pointers in C. Its the character pointers that are used in case of strings too.

Now, coming to the string, when we point a pointer to a string, by default it holds the address of the first character of the string. Lets try to understand it better.

The string, 'I am String' in memory is placed as :

```
1001 1002  1003  1004 1005 1006 1007 1008 1009 1010
I    a     m     S    t    r    i    n    g    \0
```

Since characters occupy one byte each, so they are placed like above in the memory. Note the last character, its a null character which is placed at the end of every string by default in C. This null character signifies the end of the string.

Now coming back to the point, any character pointer pointing to a string stores the address of the first character of the string. In the code above, 'ptr' holds the address of the character 'I' ie 1001. Now, when we apply the 'value of' operator '*' to 'ptr', we intend to fetch the value at address 1001 which is 'I' and hence when we print '*ptr', we get 'I' as the output.

Also, If we specify the format specifier as '%s' and use 'ptr' (which contains the starting address of the string), then the complete string is printed using printf. The concept is that %s specifier requires the address of the beginning byte of string to display the complete string, which we provided using 'ptr' (which we know holds the beginning byte address of the string). This we can see as the last print in the output above.

9.4. C-Pointer Arithmetic

A pointer in c is an address, which is a numeric value. Therefore, you can perform arithmetic operations on a pointer just as you can on a numeric value. There are four arithmetic operators that can be used on pointers: ++, --, +. To understand pointer arithmetic, let us consider that **ptr** is an integer pointer which points to the address 1000. Assuming 32-bit integers, let us perform the following arithmetic operation on the pointer.

```
ptr++
```

After the above operation, the **ptr** will point to the location 1004 because each time ptr is incremented, it will point to the next integer location which is 4 bytes next to the current location. This operation will move the pointer to the next memory location without impacting the actual value at the memory location. If **ptr** points to a character whose address is 1000, then the above operation will point to the location 1001 because the next character will be available at 1001.

Incrementing a Pointer

We prefer using a pointer in our program instead of an array because the variable pointer can be incremented, unlike the array name which cannot be incremented because it is a constant pointer. The following program increments the variable pointer to access each succeeding element of the array.

```
#include<stdio.h>
constint MAX =3;
int main (){
intvar[]={10,100,200};
int i,*ptr;
/* let us have array address in pointer */
  ptr =var;
for( i =0; i < MAX; i++){
    printf("Address of var[%d] = %x\n", i, ptr );
    printf("Value of var[%d] = %d\n", i,*ptr );
/* move to the next location */
    ptr++;
}
return0;
}
```

When the above code is compiled and executed, it produces the following result –

```
Address of var[0] = bf882b30
Value of var[0] = 10
Address of var[1] = bf882b34
Value of var[1] = 100
Address of var[2] = bf882b38
Value of var[2] = 200
```

Decrementing a Pointer

The same considerations apply to decrementing a pointer, which decreases its value by the number of bytes of its data type as shown below.

```
#include<stdio.h>
constint MAX =3;
int main (){
intvar[]={10,100,200};
int i,*ptr;
/* let us have array address in pointer */
  ptr =&var[MAX-1];
for( i = MAX; i >0; i--){
    printf("Address of var[%d] = %x\n", i-1, ptr );
    printf("Value of var[%d] = %d\n", i-1,*ptr );
/* move to the previous location */
    ptr--;
}
return0;
}
```

When the above code is compiled and executed, it produces the following result –

```
Address of var[2] = bfedbcd8
Value of var[2] = 200
Address of var[1] = bfedbcd4
Value of var[1] = 100
Address of var[0] = bfedbcd0
Value of var[0] = 10
```

Pointer Comparisons

Pointers may be compared by using relational operators, such as ==, <, and >. If p1 and p2 point to variables that are related to each other, such as elements of the same array, then p1 and p2 can be meaningfully compared.

The following program modifies the previous example – one by incrementing the variable pointer so long as the address to which it points is either less than or equal to the address of the last element of the array, which is &var[MAX - 1].

```
#include<stdio.h>
constint MAX =3;
int main (){
intvar[]={10,100,200};
int i,*ptr;
/* let us have address of the first element in pointer */
  ptr =var;
  i =0;
while( ptr <=&var[MAX -1]){
    printf("Address of var[%d] = %x\n", i, ptr );
    printf("Value of var[%d] = %d\n", i,*ptr );
/* point to the previous location */
    ptr++;
    i++;
}
return0;
}
```

When the above code is compiled and executed, it produces the following result –

```
Address of var[0] = bfdbcb20
Value of var[0] = 10
Address of var[1] = bfdbcb24
Value of var[1] = 100
Address of var[2] = bfdbcb28
Value of var[2] = 200
```

9.5. Array of Pointers

Before we understand the concept of arrays of pointers, let us consider the following example, which uses an array of 3 integers

```
#include<stdio.h>
constint MAX =3;
int main (){
intvar[]={10,100,200};
int i;
```

```
for(i =0; i < MAX; i++){
    printf("Value of var[%d] = %d\n", i,var[i]);
}
return0;
}
```

When the above code is compiled and executed, it produces the following result –

```
Value of var[0] = 10
Value of var[1] = 100
Value of var[2] = 200
```

There may be a situation when we want to maintain an array, which can store pointers to an int or char or any other data type available. Following is the declaration of an array of pointers to an integer.

```
int *ptr[MAX];
```

It declares **ptr** as an array of MAX integer pointers. Thus, each element in ptr, holds a pointer to an int value. The following example uses three integers, which are stored in an array of pointers, as follows.

```
#include<stdio.h>
constint MAX =3;
int main (){
intvar[]={10,100,200};
int i,*ptr[MAX];
for( i =0; i < MAX; i++){
    ptr[i]=&var[i];/* assign the address of integer. */
}
for( i =0; i < MAX; i++){
    printf("Value of var[%d] = %d\n", i,*ptr[i]);
}
return0;
}
```

When the above code is compiled and executed, it produces the following result.

```
Value of var[0] = 10
```

```
Value of var[1] = 100
Value of var[2] = 200
```

You can also use an array of pointers to character to store a list of strings as follows.

```
#include<stdio.h>
constint MAX =4;
int main (){
char*names[]={
"Zara Ali",
"Hina Ali",
"Nuha Ali",
"Sara Ali"
};
int i =0;
for( i =0; i < MAX; i++){
    printf("Value of names[%d] = %s\n", i, names[i]);
}
return0;
}
```

When the above code is compiled and executed, it produces the following result.

```
Value of names[0] = Zara Ali

Value of names[1] = Hina Ali

Value of names[2] = Nuha Ali

Value of names[3] = Sara Ali
```

9.6. Pointer to Pointer

A pointer to a pointer is a form of multiple indirection, or a chain of pointers. Normally, a pointer contains the address of a variable. When we define a pointer to a pointer, the first pointer contains the address of the second pointer, which points to the location that contains the actual value as shown below.

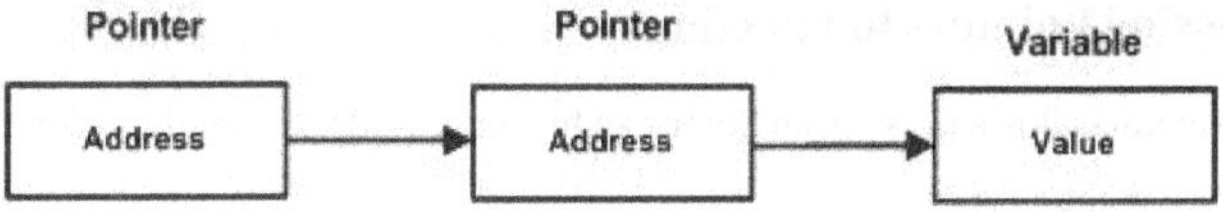

A variable that is a pointer to a pointer must be declared as such. This is done by placing an additional asterisk in front of its name. For example, the following declaration declares a pointer to a pointer of type int.

```
int **var;
```

When a target value is indirectly pointed to by a pointer to a pointer, accessing that value requires that the asterisk operator be applied twice, as is shown below in the example.

```
#include<stdio.h>
int main (){
intvar;
int*ptr;
int**pptr;
var=3000;
/* take the address of var */
  ptr =&var;
/* take the address of ptr using address of operator & */
  pptr =&ptr;
/* take the value using pptr */
  printf("Value of var = %d\n",var);
  printf("Value available at *ptr = %d\n",*ptr );
  printf("Value available at **pptr = %d\n",**pptr);
return0;
}
```

When the above code is compiled and executed, it produces the following result.

```
Value of var = 3000
Value available at *ptr = 3000
Value available at **pptr = 3000
```

9.7. Passing Pointers to Functions

C programming allows passing a pointer to a function. To do so, simply declare the function parameter as a pointer type.

Following is a simple example where we pass an unsigned long pointer to a function and change the value inside the function which reflects back in the calling function.

```
#include<stdio.h>
#include<time.h>
void getSeconds(unsignedlong*par);
int main (){
unsignedlong sec;
  getSeconds(&sec );
/* print the actual value */
  printf("Number of seconds: %ld\n", sec );
return0;
}
void getSeconds(unsignedlong*par){
/* get the current number of seconds */
*par = time( NULL );
return;
}
```

When the above code is compiled and executed, it produces the following result.

```
Number of seconds :1294450468
```

The function, which can accept a pointer, can also accept an array as shown in the following example.

```
#include<stdio.h>
/* function declaration */
double getAverage(int*arr,int size);
int main (){
/* an int array with 5 elements */
int balance[5]={1000,2,3,17,50};
double avg;
/* pass pointer to the array as an argument */
```

```
  avg = getAverage( balance,5);
/* output the returned value  */
  printf("Average value is: %f\n", avg );
return0;
}
double getAverage(int*arr,int size){
int  i, sum =0;
double avg;
for(i =0; i < size;++i){
    sum += arr[i];
}
  avg =(double)sum / size;
return avg;
}
```

When the above code is compiled together and executed, it produces the following result.

```
Average value is: 214.40000
```

Return Pointer from Functions in C

We have seen in the last chapter how C programming allows to return an array from a function. Similarly, C also allows to return a pointer from a function. To do so, you would have to declare a function returning a pointer as in the following example.

```
int* myFunction(){
.
.
.
}
```

Second point to remember is that, it is not a good idea to return the address of a local variable outside the function, so you would have to define the local variable as **static** variable.

Now, consider the following function which will generate 10 random numbers and return them using an array name which represents a pointer, i.e., address of first array element.

```
#include<stdio.h>
#include<time.h>
```

```
/* function to generate and return random numbers. */
int* getRandom(){
staticint r[10];
int i;
/* set the seed */
  srand((unsigned)time( NULL ));
for( i =0; i <10;++i){
    r[i]= rand();
    printf("%d\n", r[i]);
}
return r;
}
/* main function to call above defined function */
int main (){
/* a pointer to an int */
int*p;
int i;
  p = getRandom();
for( i =0; i <10; i++){
    printf("*(p + [%d]) : %d\n", i,*(p + i));
}
return0;
}
```

When the above code is compiled together and executed, it produces the following result.

```
1523198053
1187214107
1108300978
430494959
1421301276
930971084
123250484
106932140
1604461820
```

```
149169022
*(p + [0]) : 1523198053
*(p + [1]) : 1187214107
*(p + [2]) : 1108300978
*(p + [3]) : 430494959
*(p + [4]) : 1421301276
*(p + [5]) : 930971084
*(p + [6]) : 123250484
*(p + [7]) : 106932140
*(p + [8]) : 1604461820
*(p + [9]) : 149169022
```

9.8. Void Pointer

A void pointer is a pointer that has no associated data type with it. A void pointer can hold address of any type and can be typcasted to any type.

```
int a = 10;
char b = 'x';
void *p = &a; // void pointer holds address of int 'a'
p = &b; // void pointer holds address of char 'b'
```

Advantages of Void Pointers

1) malloc() and calloc() return void * type and this allows these functions to be used to allocate memory of any data type (just because of void *)

```
int main(void)
{
   // Note that malloc() returns void * which can be
   // typecasted to any type like int *, char *, ..
   int *x = malloc(sizeof(int) * n);
}
```

Note that the above program compiles in C, but doesn't compile in C++. In C++, we must explicitly typecast return value of malloc to (int *).

2) void pointers in C are used to implement generic functions in C. For example compare function which is used in qsort().

Some Interesting Facts

1) void pointers cannot be dereferenced. For example the following program doesn't compile.

```
#include<stdio.h>
intmain()
{
  inta = 10;
  void*ptr = &a;
  printf("%d", *ptr);
  return0;
}
```

Output

```
Compiler Error: 'void*' is not a pointer-to-object type
```

The following program compiles and runs fine.

```
#include<stdio.h>
int main()
{
  int a = 10;
  void *ptr = &a;
  printf("%d", *(int *)ptr);
  return 0;
}
```

Output

```
10
```

2) The C standard doesn't allow pointer arithmetic with void pointers. However, in GNU C it is allowed by considering the size of void is 1. For example the following program compiles and runs fine in gcc.

```
#include<stdio.h>
intmain()
{
  inta[2] = {1, 2};
  void*ptr = &a;
  ptr = ptr + sizeof(int);
  printf("%d", *(int*)ptr);
```

```
    return0;
}
```

Output

```
2
```

Note that the above program may not work in other compilers.

Summary : Void Pointer

Scenario	Behavior
When We assign address of integer variable to void pointer	Void Pointer Becomes Integer Pointer
When We assign address of character variable to void pointer	Void Pointer Becomes Character Pointer
When We assign address of floating variable to void pointer	Void Pointer Becomes Floating Pointer

What are Near, Far and Huge Pointers?

These are some old concepts used in 16 bit intel architectures in the days of MS DOS, not much useful anymore.

- **Near pointer** is used to store 16 bit addresses means within current segment on a 16 bit machine. The limitation is that we can only access 64kb of data at a time.
- **A far pointer** is typically 32 bit that can access memory outside current segment. To use this, compiler allocates a segment register to store segment address, then another register to store offset within current segment.
- Like far pointer, **huge pointer** is also typically 32 bit and can access outside segment. In case of far pointers, a segment is fixed. In far pointer, the segment part cannot be modified, but in Huge it can be.

Difference between a Far Pointer and a Near Pointer

In a near pointer, it uses offset data address in a segment default while a far pointer uses both sector data address and offset data address and it locates the data in the computer memory.

9.9. Dangling Pointer

1. Dangling pointers arise when an object is deleted or de-allocated, without modifying the value of the pointer, so that the pointer still points to the memory location of the de-allocated memory.
2. In short pointer pointing to non-existing memory location is called dangling pointer.

Examples of Dangling Pointer

There are different ways where Pointer acts as dangling pointer.

Way 1: Using Free or De-Allocating Memory

```
#include<stdlib.h>
{
char *ptr = malloc(Constant_Value);
  .......
  .......
  .......
  free (ptr);     /* ptr now becomes a dangling pointer */
}
```

We have declared the character pointer in the first step. After execution of some statements we have de-allocated memory which is allocated previously for the pointer.

As soon as memory is de-allocated for pointer, pointer becomes dangling pointer

Problem: If any pointer is pointing the memory address of any variable but after some variable has deleted from that memory location while pointer is still pointing such memory location. Such pointer is known as **dangling pointer** and this problem is known as **dangling pointer problem.**

How to Ensure that Pointer is no Longer Dangling ?

```
#include<stdlib.h>
{
  char *ptr = malloc(Constant_Value);
  .......
  .......
  .......
  free (ptr); /* ptr now becomes a dangling pointer */
  ptr = NULL   /* ptr is no more dangling pointer */
}
```

After de-allocating memory, initialize pointer to NULL so that pointer will be no longer dangling.

Assigning NULL value means pointer is not pointing to any memory location

Way 2: Out of Scope

```
#include<stdlib.h>
void main()
{
  char *ptr = NULL;
  .....
  .....
  {
    char ch;
    ptr = &ch;
  }
  ..... /* dp is now a dangling pointer */
}
```

1. Character Pointer is Declared in the first Step.
2. Pointer Variable 'ptr' is pointing to Character Variable 'ch' **declared in the inner block**.
3. As character variable is non-visible in Outer Block , then Pointer is Still Pointing to Same Invalid memory location in Outer block , then Pointer becomes **"Dangling".**

Way 3: Function Call

```
int * func ( void )
{
   int num = 14;
   /* ... */
   return &num;
}
```

Attempts to read from the pointer may still return the correct value (1234) for a while after calling func, but any functions called thereafter will overwrite the stack storage allocated for num with other values and the pointer would no longer work correctly.

If a pointer to num must be returned, num must have scope beyond the function—it might be declared as static.

9.10. Wild Pointer

A pointer which has not been initialized to anything (not even NULL) is known as wild pointer. The pointer may be initialized to a non-NULL garbage value that may not be a valid address.

```
intmain()
{
  int*p;  /* wild pointer */
   intx = 10;
   // p is not a wild pointer now
  p = &x;
   return0;
    }
```

9.11. Exercises

1) What will be the output of the C program?

```
#include<stdio.h>
int main(){
        int a = 130;
        char *ptr;
        ptr = (char *)&a;
        printf("%d ",*ptr);
        return 0;
}
```

A. -126

B. Run Time Error

C. Garbage value

D. Compile Time Error

Answer

Option: A

Explanation

Here a variable a holds the value 130 of integer data types, which is then type casted to char data types using pointer variable. As we know that a value 130 is exceeding the char range (-128 to 127), thus it loops through its range.

For Example

128 = -128

129 = -127

130 = -126

140 = -125

2) What will be the output of the C program?

```
#include<stdio.h>
int main(){
        int i = 3;
        int *j;
        int **k;
        j = &i;
        k = &j;
        k++;
        printf("%d ",**k);
        return 0;
}
```

A. Garbage value

B. Compilation Error

C. Run time error

D. Linker Error

Answer

Option: C

Explanation

Here k is the pointer variable which holds the address of another pointer variable j. where j is also a pointer variable which also holds the address of another variable i. Now when the address of a pointer variable k is incremented by 1, then k hold some other garbage value which is not the address of any other variable. Thus runtime error occurs.

3) What will be the output of the C program?

```
#include<stdio.h>
int main(){
        int i = 3;
        int *j;
        j = &i;
        j++;
        printf("%d ",*j);
```

```
        return 0;
}
```

A. Linker Error

B. Run time error

C. Compilation Error

D. Garbage value

Answer

Option: D

Explanation

Here j is the pointer variable which holds the address of another variable called i. When j is incremented, the address stored in j is incremented. As a result some garbage value will be displayed as we had not initialized anything to the address next to the address of a variable i.

4) What will be the output of the C program?

```
#include<stdio.h>
#include<string.h>
int main(){
        char *ptr = "hello";
        char a[22];
        strcpy(a, "world");
        printf("\n%s %s",ptr, a);
        return 0;
}
```

A. hello world

B. Run time error

C. Compilation Error

D. Garbage value

Answer

Option: A

Explanation

Simply, pointer variable ptr is initialized with the char string "hello" and a normal variable a is set to copy the string "world" using the inbuilt function strcpy. Thus it displayed hello world.

5) What will be the output of the C program?

```
#include<stdio.h>
#include<string.h>
int main(){
        char *ptr = "hello";
        char a[22];
        *ptr = "world";
        printf("\n%s %s",ptr, a);
        return 0;
}
```

A. Linker Error

B. Run time error

C. Compilation Error

D. Garbage value

Answer

Option: C

Explanation

ptr is a pointer variable of character data type, string "world" can be set to the pointer variable ptr only at the initializing time.

6) What will be the output of the C program?

```
#include<stdio.h>
int main()
{
        char *ptr = "helloworld";
        printf(ptr + 4);
        return 0;
}
```

A. oworld

B. world

C. hell

D. hello

Answer

Option: A

Explanation

Here the characters in string "helloworld" is placed in address as follows. ptr +4 tells the compiler to start reading from 4th place of a string "Helloworld".

Character	Address
h	4214784
e	4214785
l	4214786
l	4214787
o	4214788
w	4214789
o	4214790
r	4214791
l	4214792
d	4214793

7) What will be the output of the C program?

```
#include<stdio.h>

#include<string.h>

int main(){

        register a = 1;

        int far *ptr;

        ptr = &a;

        printf("%u",ptr);

        return 0;

}
```

A. Address of a

B. Run time error

C. Garbage value

D. Compile time error

Answer

Option: D

Explanation

"a" is a register variable which holds a value 1.

It must be noted that variable a hold its value 1 in a register but not in computer memory location thus the pointer variable ptr cannot hold the address of a.

8) What will be the output of the C program?

```
#include<stdio.h>
#include<string.h>
int main(){
        char a = 30, b = 5;
        char *p = &a, *q = &b;
        printf("%d", p - q);
        return 0;
}
```

A. 1

B. Run time error

C. Compilation Error

D. 25

Answer

Option: A

Explanation

Difference between any two variables of same data type are always one.

9) What will be the output of the C program?

```
#include<stdio.h>
int main(){
        int *ptr, b;
        b = sizeof(ptr);
        printf("%d" , b);
        return 0;
}
```

A. 2

B. 4

C. Compilation Error

D. Run time error

Answer

Option: B

Explanation

Since ptr is a pointer variable of integer data types.

10) What will be the output of the C program?

```
#include<stdio.h>
struct classroom
{
	int students[7];
};
int main()
{
	struct classroom cr = {2, 3, 5, 7, 11, 13};
	int *ptr;
	ptr = (int *)&cr;
	printf("%d",*(ptr + 4));
	return 0;
}
```

A. 5

B. 11

C. 13

D. 7

Answer

Option: B

Explanation

Here a pointer variable ptr holds the address of a first value (2) of an object cr, then the address of the pointer variable is incremented by 4 and then its value is displayed.

For Example

```
*(ptr + 0) = 2
*(ptr + 1) = 3
*(ptr + 2) = 5
*(ptr + 3) = 7
*(ptr + 4) = 11
*(ptr + 5) = 13
```

11) What will be the output of the C program?

```
#include<stdio.h>
unsigned long int (*function())[5]{
        static unsigned long int arr[5] = {2, 3, 5, 7, 11};
        printf("%d", *arr);
        return &arr;
}
int main(){
        unsigned long int (*ptr)[5];
        ptr = function();
        printf("%d", *(*ptr + 4));
        return 0;
}
```

A. 2, 5

B. 2, 7

C. 2, 11

D. Compilation error

Answer

Option: C

Explanation

Simply, function holds an array which returns the address of first element in an array arr.

Note: ptr itself an address which holds the address of first element in an array arr. Thus *ptr returns the address of a first element in an array arr and then **ptr returns the value for the first element in an array arr, as per our "printf(",%d",*(*ptr+4));" returns a value 11 inside an array arr.

12) What will be the output of the C program?

```
#include<stdio.h>
int main(){
        int a = 25, b;
        int *ptr, *ptr1;
        ptr = &a;
        ptr1 = &b;
```

```
        b = 36;
        printf("%d %d",*ptr, *ptr1);
        return 0;
}
```

A. 25 45632845

B. Run time error

C. Compilation Error

D. 25 36

Answer

Option: D

Explanation

ptr holds the address of a variable A and ptr1 holds the address of a variable B . The value ofA is 25 and B is 36.

13) What will be the output of the C program?

```
#include<stdio.h>
int main(){
        int * ptr ;
        printf("%d", sizeof(ptr));
        return 0;
}
```

A. 4

B. 8

C. 2

D. compilation error

Answer

Option: A

Explanation

Size of int is 4 in 32 bits and 64bit operating system.

14) What will be the output of the C program?

```
#include<stdio.h>
int main(){
        int *ptr = 2;
        printf("%d", sizeof(ptr));
        return 0;
}
```

A. Garbage value

B. 2

C. Compilation error

D. 4

Answer

Option: C

Explanation

ptr is the pointer variable of integer data type. Thus ptr cannot be initialized by any integer value other than 0.

15) What will be the output of the C program?

```
#include<stdio.h>
int main(){
        int *ptr;
        *ptr = 5;
        printf("%d" , *ptr);
        return 0;
}
```

A. compilation error

B. Runtime error

C. 5

D. linker error

Answer

Option: B

Explanation

Pointer variable (*ptr) cannot be initialized.

16) What will be the output of the C program?

```
#include<stdio.h>
int main(){
        int a = 36;
        int *ptr;
        ptr = &a;
        printf("%u %u", *&ptr , &*ptr);
        return 0;
}
```

A. Address Value

B. Value Address

C. Address Address

D. Compilation error

Answer

Option: C

Explanation

& and * cancelled each other and display the address stored in a pointer variable ptr i.e) the address of a.

17) What will be the output of the C program?

```
#include<stdio.h>
int main(){
        int num = 10;
        printf("num = %d addresss of num = %u",num, &num);
        num++;
        printf("\n num = %d addresss of num = %u",num, &num);
        return 0;
}
```

A. Compilation error

B. num = 10 address of num = 2293436
num = 11 address of num = 2293438

C. num = 10 address of num = 2293436
num = 11 address of num = 2293440

D. num = 10 address of num = 2293436

num = 11 address of num = 2293436

Answer

Option: D

Explanation

Here a variable num holds the value 10 and get its address as 2293436, then increment is done as num++ which uses the same address space to store the incremented value.

18) What will be the output of the C program?

```
#include<stdio.h>
int main(){
        int i = 25;
        int *j;
        int **k;
        j = &i;
        k = &j;
        printf("%u %u %u ",k,*k,**k);
        return 0;
}
```

A. address address value

B. address value value

C. address address address

D. compilation error

Answer

Option: A

Explanation

Here a pointer variable *j hold the address of i and then another pointer variable *k hold the address of j.

Now

k = address of j

*k = address of i

**k = value of i.

19) What will be the output of the C program?

```
#include<stdio.h>
int main()
{
        int a, b, c;
        char *p = 0;
        int *q = 0;
        double *r = 0;
        a = (int)(p + 1);
        b = (int)(q + 1);
        c = (int)(r + 1);
        printf("%d %d  %d",a, b, c);
        return 0;
}
```

A. Runtime error

B. 0 0 0

C. Compilation error

D. 1 4 8

Answer

Option: D

Explanation

Initializing pointer variable to zero is possible. Since initial address of any data type is zero, So its next address will be size of data type.

Here a pointer variable *p belongs to char data type, thus a = (int) (p + 1); increase its address by 1 as it belongs to char datatype. Thus variable a = 1 .

Here a pointer variable *q belongs to int data type, thus b = (int) (q + 1); increase its address by 4 as it belongs to int datatype. Thus variable b = 4 .

Here a pointer variable *r belongs to double data type, thus c = (int) (r + 1); increase its address by 8 as it belongs to double datatype. Thus variable c = 8 .

20) What will be the output of the C program?

```
#include<stdio.h>
int main()
{
        const int a = 5;
        const int *ptr;
        ptr = &a;
        *ptr = 10;
        printf("%d\n", a);
        return 0;
}
```

A. Compilation error

B. Garbage Value

C. Address

D. 5

Answer

Option: C

Explanation

Pointer variable *ptr cannot be initialized at any time.

21) What will be the output of the C program?

```
#include<stdio.h>
int main()
{
        printf("%d", sizeof(void *));
        return 0;
}
```

A. 1

B. compilation error

C. Runtime error

D. 4

Answer

Option: D

Explanation

Size of void is 1 and the sizeof void pointer is 4.

22) What will be the output of the C program?

```
#include<stdio.h>
void function(char**);
int main()
{
        char *arr[] = { "ant", "bat", "cat", "dog", "egg", "fly" };
        function(arr);
        return 0;
}
void function(char **ptr)
{
        char *ptr1;
        ptr1 = (ptr += sizeof(int))[-2];
        printf("%s\n", ptr1);
}
```

A. cat

B. bat

C. dog

D. egg

Answer

Option: A

Explanation

Here function() gives the address of first value("ant") in an arr. This address is summationed by a sizeof(int) which is 4. now the address in ptr points the value eggs, which is then reduced by 2 . now it points to the value cat which is finally displayed

Try By Yourself

1) What will be the output of the C program?

```
#include<stdio.h>
int main(){
        char *ptr = "Pointer in c", arr[15];
        arr[15] = *ptr;
        printf("%c",arr[0]);
        return 0;
}
```

A. Garbage value

B. Run time error

C. P

D. Compile time error

2) What will be the output of the C program?

```
#include<stdio.h>
int main(){
 char arr[15] = "pointer array";
 int *ptr;
 ptr = arr;
 printf("%c",ptr[1]);
 return 0;
}
```

A. Garbage value

B. o

C. t

D. Compile time error

3) What will be the output of the C program?

```
#include<stdio.h>
int main()
{
 int a = 10, b = 6;
 int *ptr;
 ptr = &b;
 printf(" %d ", a **ptr);
 return 0;
}
```

A. Pointer type error

B. Run time error

C. Compilation error

D. 60

4) What will be the output of the C program?

```
#include<stdio.h>
int main()
{
 int *iptr;
 int i, arr[2][2] = {10, 11, 12, 13};
 iptr = *arr ;
 printf("%d ", *(iptr+2));
 return 0;
}
```

A. 12

B. 13

C. Compilation Error

D. Garbage value

5) What will be the output of the C program?

```
#include<stdio.h>

int main()

{

char *cities[] = {"Delhi", "London", "Sydney"};

int **i = &cities[0];

printf("%c\n", **i);

return 0;

}
```

A. Delhi

B. Garbage address

C. D

D. Compile Time Error

6) What will be the output of the C program?

```
#include<stdio.h>
int main(){
 char *cities[] = {"UAE", "Spain", "America"};
 int **i = &cities[0];
 int **j = &cities[1];
 int **k = &cities[2];
 printf("%c%c%c\n", **i,**j,**k);
```

```
return 0;
}
```

A. Upa

B. USA

C. UAE

D. None of the above

7) What will be the output of the C program?

```
#include<stdio.h>
int main(){
 char array[5] = "Knot", *ptr, i, *ptr1;
 ptr = &array[1];
 ptr1 = ptr + 3;
 *ptr1 = 101;
 for(i = 0; i < 4;i++)
 printf("%c", *ptr++);
 return 0;
}
```

A. not

B. Knot

C. note

D. garbage value

8) What will be the output of the C program?

```
#include<stdio.h>
int main()
{
	char *ptr = "Pointer-to-String", i;
	printf("%s", ++ptr);
	return 0;
}
```

A. Pointer-to-String

B. o

C. ointer-to-String

D. None of the above

9) What will be the output of the C program?

```
#include<stdio.h>
```

```
int main()
{
        char *str = "His";
        int i;
        for(i = 0; i < strlen(str); i++)
        printf("%s", str++);
        return 0;
}
```

A. Hisis

B. Hisiss

C. HisHisHis

D. None of the above

10) What will be the output of the C program?

```
#include<stdio.h>
int main()
{
        char arr[10] = "Mango", *ptr;
        ptr = (&arr[1]++);
        printf("%s",ptr++);
        return 0;
}
```

A. ango

B. ngo

C. Compile time error

D. Mango

11) What will be the output of the C program?

```
#include<stdio.h>
int main(){
 int i = 5;
 void *vptr;
 vptr = &i;
 printf("\nValue of iptr = %d ", *vptr);
```

```
 return 0;
}
```

A. 5

B. garbage address

C. garbage value

D. Compile time error

12) Fill the question mark to get "void pointer" as an output?

```
#include<stdio.h>
int main(){
 char *ptr = "void pointer";
 void *vptr;
 vptr = &ptr;
 printf("%s" , ?);
 return 0;
}
```

A. *(char **)vptr

B. (char **)vptr

C. *(char *)vptr

D. (char *)vptr

13) What will be the output of the C program?

```
#include<stdio.h>
#define NULL "error";
int main()
{
 char *ptr = NULL;
 printf("%s",ptr);
 return 0;
}
```

A. Run time error

B. NULL

C. error

D. Compile time error

14) Fill the question mark to get "5" as an output?

```
#include<stdio.h>
int main()
{
 int i = 5,*ptr;
 ptr= &i;
 void *vptr;
 vptr = &ptr;
 printf("\nValue of iptr = %d ", ?);
 return 0;
}
```

A. **(int **)vptr

B. **(int ***)vptr

C. **(int ****)vptr

D. All the above

Answer

1) a 2) c 3)d 4)a 5)c 6)b 7)c 8)c 9)a 10)c 11)d 12)a 13)c 14)d

CHAPTER 10

C STRUCTURE

10.1. Introduction to C Structure

When you design a program, it is important to choose an optimal way to represent the data that the program processes. In simple cases, scalar variables and arrays are sufficient. However in practical programming context, you need a new form of variable that reflects the real world. For example, in your program, you may want to refer to an address that holds multiple fields including house number, street, zip code, state and country.

C provides a special kind of variable called *structure*. C structure allows you to wrap related variables that has different data types into a single variable. A structure can contain any valid data types such as int, char, float, array, pointer or even other structures. Each variable in the structure is called structure member.

10.2. Defining a Structure

To define a structure, you must use the **struct** statement. The struct statement defines a new data type, with more than one member. The format of the struct statement is as follows

```
struct[structure tag]{
  member definition;
  member definition;
...
  member definition;
}[one or more structure variables];
```

The **structure tag** is optional and each member definition is a normal variable definition, such as int i; or float f; or any other valid variable definition. At the end of the structure's definition, before the final semicolon, you can specify one or more structure variables but it is optional. Here is the way you would declare the Book structure

```
structBooks{
char title[50];
char author[50];
char subject[100];
int  book_id;
} book;
```

Accessing Structure Members

To access any member of a structure, we use the **member access operator (.)**. The member access operator is coded as a period between the structure variable name and the structure member that we wish to access. You would use the keyword **struct** to define variables of structure type. The following example shows how to use a structure in a program.

```
#include<stdio.h>
#include<string.h>
structBooks{
char title[50];
char author[50];
char subject[100];
int  book_id;
};
int main(){
structBooksBook1;/* Declare Book1 of type Book */
structBooksBook2;/* Declare Book2 of type Book */
/* book 1 specification */
  strcpy(Book1.title,"C Programming");
  strcpy(Book1.author,"Nuha Ali");
  strcpy(Book1.subject,"C Programming Tutorial");
Book1.book_id =6495407;
/* book 2 specification */
  strcpy(Book2.title,"Telecom Billing");
  strcpy(Book2.author,"Zara Ali");
  strcpy(Book2.subject,"Telecom Billing Tutorial");
Book2.book_id =6495700;
/* print Book1 info */
  printf("Book 1 title : %s\n",Book1.title);
  printf("Book 1 author : %s\n",Book1.author);
  printf("Book 1 subject : %s\n",Book1.subject);
  printf("Book 1 book_id : %d\n",Book1.book_id);
/* print Book2 info */
  printf("Book 2 title : %s\n",Book2.title);
  printf("Book 2 author : %s\n",Book2.author);
```

```
  printf("Book 2 subject : %s\n",Book2.subject);
  printf("Book 2 book_id : %d\n",Book2.book_id);
return0;
}
```

When the above code is compiled and executed, it produces the following result –

```
Book 1 title : C Programming
Book 1 author : Nuha Ali
Book 1 subject : C Programming Tutorial
Book 1 book_id : 6495407
Book 2 title : Telecom Billing
Book 2 author : Zara Ali
Book 2 subject : Telecom Billing Tutorial
Book 2 book_id : 6495700
```

10.3. Structures as Function Arguments

You can pass a structure as a function argument in the same way as you pass any other variable or pointer.

```
#include<stdio.h>
#include<string.h>
structBooks{
char  title[50];
char  author[50];
char  subject[100];
int   book_id;
};
/* function declaration */
void printBook(structBooks book );
int main(){
structBooksBook1;/* Declare Book1 of type Book */
structBooksBook2;/* Declare Book2 of type Book */
/* book 1 specification */
  strcpy(Book1.title,"C Programming");
  strcpy(Book1.author,"Nuha Ali");
```

```
  strcpy(Book1.subject,"C Programming Tutorial");
Book1.book_id =6495407;
/* book 2 specification */
  strcpy(Book2.title,"Telecom Billing");
  strcpy(Book2.author,"Zara Ali");
  strcpy(Book2.subject,"Telecom Billing Tutorial");
Book2.book_id =6495700;
/* print Book1 info */
  printBook(Book1);
/* Print Book2 info */
  printBook(Book2);
return0;
}
void printBook(structBooks book ){
  printf("Book title : %s\n", book.title);
  printf("Book author : %s\n", book.author);
  printf("Book subject : %s\n", book.subject);
  printf("Book book_id : %d\n", book.book_id);
}
```

When the above code is compiled and executed, it produces the following result –

```
Book title : C Programming
Book author : Nuha Ali
Book subject : C Programming Tutorial
Book book_id : 6495407
Book title : Telecom Billing
Book author : Zara Ali
Book subject : Telecom Billing Tutorial
Book book_id : 6495700
```

10.4. Pointers to Structures

You can define pointers to structures in the same way as you define pointer to any other variable.

```
struct Books *struct_pointer;
```

Now, you can store the address of a structure variable in the above defined pointer variable. To find the address of a structure variable, place the '&'; operator before the structure's name as follows.

```
struct_pointer =&Book1;
```

To access the members of a structure using a pointer to that structure, you must use the → operator as follows.

```
struct_pointer->title;
```

Let us re-write the above example using structure pointer.

```
#include<stdio.h>
#include<string.h>
structBooks{
char  title[50];
char  author[50];
char  subject[100];
int   book_id;
};
/* function declaration */
void printBook(structBooks*book );
int main(){
structBooksBook1;/* Declare Book1 of type Book */
structBooksBook2;/* Declare Book2 of type Book */
/* book 1 specification */
  strcpy(Book1.title,"C Programming");
  strcpy(Book1.author,"Nuha Ali");
  strcpy(Book1.subject,"C Programming Tutorial");
Book1.book_id =6495407;
/* book 2 specification */
  strcpy(Book2.title,"Telecom Billing");
  strcpy(Book2.author,"Zara Ali");
  strcpy(Book2.subject,"Telecom Billing Tutorial");
Book2.book_id =6495700;
```

```
/* print Book1 info by passing address of Book1 */
  printBook(&Book1);
/* print Book2 info by passing address of Book2 */
  printBook(&Book2);
return0;
}
void printBook(structBooks*book ){
  printf("Book title : %s\n", book->title);
  printf("Book author : %s\n", book->author);
  printf("Book subject : %s\n", book->subject);
  printf("Book book_id : %d\n", book->book_id);
}
```

When the above code is compiled and executed, it produces the following result –

```
Book title : C Programming
Book author : Nuha Ali
Book subject : C Programming Tutorial
Book book_id : 6495407
Book title : Telecom Billing
Book author : Zara Ali
Book subject : Telecom Billing Tutorial
Book book_id : 6495700
```

10.5. Bit Fields

Bit Fields allow the packing of data in a structure. This is especially useful when memory or data storage is at a premium. Typical examples include.

- Packing several objects into a machine word. e.g. 1 bit flags can be compacted.
- Reading external file formats -- non-standard file formats could be read in, e.g., 9-bit integers.

C allows us to do this in a structure definition by putting :bit length after the variable. For example.

```
struct packed_struct {
unsignedint f1:1;
unsignedint f2:1;
unsignedint f3:1;
```

```
unsignedint f4:1;
unsignedint type:4;
unsignedint my_int:9;
} pack;
```

Here, the packed_struct contains 6 members: Four 1 bit flags f1..f3, a 4-bit type and a 9-bit my_int.

C automatically packs the above bit fields as compactly as possible, provided that the maximum length of the field is less than or equal to the integer word length of the computer. If this is not the case, then some compilers may allow memory overlap for the fields while others would store the next field in the next word.

Example of Structure

Write a C program to add two distances entered by user. Measurement of distance should be in inch and feet. (Note: 12 inches = 1 foot)

```
#include<stdio.h>
structDistance
{
int feet;
float inch;
} dist1, dist2, sum;
int main()
{
  printf("1st distance\n");
// Input of feet for structure variable dist1
  printf("Enter feet: ");
  scanf("%d",&dist1.feet);
// Input of inch for structure variable dist1
  printf("Enter inch: ");
  scanf("%f",&dist1.inch);
  printf("2nd distance\n");
// Input of feet for structure variable dist2
  printf("Enter feet: ");
  scanf("%d",&dist2.feet);
// Input of feet for structure variable dist2
  printf("Enter inch: ");
  scanf("%f",&dist2.inch);
  sum.feet = dist1.feet + dist2.feet;
  sum.inch = dist1.inch + dist2.inch;
if(sum.inch >12)
```

```
{
            //If inch is greater than 12, changing it to feet.
++sum.feet;
    sum.inch = sum.inch -12;
}
// printing sum of distance dist1 and dist2
  printf("Sum of distances = %d\'-%.1f\"", sum.feet, sum.inch);
return0;
}
```

Output

```
1st distance
Enter feet: 12
Enter inch: 7.9
2nd distance
Enter feet: 2
Enter inch: 9.8
Sum of distances = 15'-5.7"
```

Structure Normal Variable vs Pointer Variable

Using normal variable	Using pointer variable

Syntax:
struct tag_name
{
data type var_name1;
data type var_name2;
data type var_name3;
};
	Syntax:
	struct tag_name
	{
	data type var_name1;
	data type var_name2;
	data type var_name3;
	};

Example:
struct student
{
int mark;
char name[10];
float average;
};
	Example:
	struct student
	{
	int mark;
	char name[10];
	float average;
	};

Declaring structure using normal variable: struct student report;	**Declaring structure using pointer variable:** struct student *report, rep;
Initializing structure using normal variable: struct student report = {100, "Mani", 99.5};	**Initializing structure using pointer variable:** struct student rep = {100, "Mani", 99.5}; report = &rep;
Accessing structure members using normal variable: report.mark; report.name; report.average;	**Accessing structure members using pointer variable:** report -> mark; report -> name; report -> average;

10.6. Structure within Structure

- Nested structure in C is nothing but structure within structure. One structure can be declared inside other structure as we declare structure members inside a structure.
- The structure variables can be a normal structure variable or a pointer variable to access the data. You can learn below concepts in this section.

1. Structure within structure in C using normal variable.
2. Structure within structure in C using pointer variable.

1) Structure within Structure in c Using Normal Variable

- This program explains how to use structure within structure in C using normal variable. "student_college_detail' structure is declared inside "student_detail" structure in this program. Both structure variables are normal structure variables.
- Please note that members of "student_college_detail" structure are accessed by 2 dot(.) operator and members of "student_detail" structure are accessed by single dot(.) operator.

Example

```
#include <stdio.h>
#include <string.h>
struct student_college_detail
{
  int college_id;
  char college_name[50];
};
struct student_detail
{
  int id;
  char name[20];
  float percentage;
  // structure within structure
  struct student_college_detail clg_data;
}stu_data;
int main()
{
  struct student_detail stu_data = {1, "Raju", 90.5, 71145,
```

```
                    "Anna University"};
    printf(" Id is: %d \n", stu_data.id);
    printf(" Name is: %s \n", stu_data.name);
    printf(" Percentage is: %f \n\n", stu_data.percentage);

    printf(" College Id is: %d \n",
            stu_data.clg_data.college_id);
    printf(" College Name is: %s \n",
            stu_data.clg_data.college_name);
    return 0;
  }
```

Output

```
Id is: 1
Name is: Raju
Percentage is: 90.500000
College Id is: 71145
College Name is: Christ University
```

2) Structure Within Structure in C Using Pointer Variable

- This program explains how to use structure within structure in C using pointer variable. "student_college_detail' structure is declared inside "student_detail" structure in this program. one normal structure variable and one pointer structure variable is used in this program.
- Please note that combination of .(dot) and ->(arrow) operators are used to access the structure member which is declared inside the structure.

Example

```
#include <stdio.h>
#include <string.h>
struct student_college_detail
{
  int college_id;
  char college_name[50];
};
```

```
struct student_detail
{
  int id;
  char name[20];
  float percentage;
  // structure within structure
  struct student_college_detail clg_data;
}stu_data, *stu_data_ptr;
int main()
{
  struct student_detail stu_data = {1, "Raju", 90.5, 71145,
                        "Anna University"};
  stu_data_ptr = &stu_data;
  printf(" Id is: %d \n", stu_data_ptr->id);
  printf(" Name is: %s \n", stu_data_ptr->name);
  printf(" Percentage is: %f \n\n",
              stu_data_ptr->percentage);
  printf(" College Id is: %d \n",
              stu_data_ptr->clg_data.college_id);
  printf(" College Name is: %s \n",
             stu_data_ptr->clg_data.college_name);
  return 0;
}
```

Output

```
Id is: 1
Name is: Raju
Percentage is: 90.500000
College Id is: 71145
College Name is: Christ University
```

10.7. Structure Padding

- In order to align the data in memory, one or more empty bytes (addresses) are inserted (or left empty) between memory addresses which are allocated for other structure members while memory allocation. This concept is called structure padding.

- Architecture of a computer processor is such a way that it can read 1 word (4 byte in 32 bit processor) from memory at a time.
- To make use of this advantage of processor, data are always aligned as 4 bytes package which leads to insert empty addresses between other member's address.
- Because of this structure padding concept in C, size of the structure is always not same as what we think.

For example, please consider below structure that has 5 members.

```
struct student
{
    int id1;
    int id2;
    char a;
    char b;
    float percentage;
};..
```

- As per C concepts, int and float datatypes occupy 4 bytes each and char datatype occupies 1 byte for 32 bit processor. So, only 14 bytes (4+4+1+1+4) should be allocated for above structure.
- But, this is wrong. Do you know why?
- Architecture of a computer processor is such a way that it can read 1 word from memory at a time.
- 1 word is equal to 4 bytes for 32 bit processor and 8 bytes for 64 bit processor. So, 32 bit processor always reads 4 bytes at a time and 64 bit processor always reads 8 bytes at a time.
- This concept is very useful to increase the processor speed.
- To make use of this advantage, memory is arranged as a group of 4 bytes in 32 bit processor and 8 bytes in 64 bit processor.
- Below C program is compiled and executed in 32 bit compiler. Please check memory allocated for structure1 and structure2 in below program.

Example

```
#include <stdio.h>
#include <string.h>
 /* Below structure1 and structure2 are same.
```

```
  They differ only in member's allignment */
 struct structure1
{
     int id1;
     int id2;
     char name;
     char c;
     float percentage;
};
 struct structure2
{
     int id1;
     char name;
     int id2;
     char c;
     float percentage;
};
 int main()
{
   struct structure1 a;
   struct structure2 b;
    printf("size of structure1 in bytes : %d\n",
         sizeof(a));
   printf ( "\n  Address of id1       = %u", &a.id1 );
   printf ( "\n  Address of id2       = %u", &a.id2 );
   printf ( "\n  Address of name      = %u", &a.name );
   printf ( "\n  Address of c         = %u", &a.c );
   printf ( "\n  Address of percentage = %u",
              &a.percentage );
    printf("  \n\nsize of structure2 in bytes : %d\n",
              sizeof(b));
   printf ( "\n  Address of id1       = %u", &b.id1 );
   printf ( "\n  Address of name      = %u", &b.name );
   printf ( "\n  Address of id2       = %u", &b.id2 );
```

```
    printf ( "\n  Address of c        = %u", &b.c );
    printf ( "\n  Address of percentage = %u",
            &b.percentage );
    getchar();
    return 0;
}
```

Output

```
size of structure1 in bytes : 16
Address of id1 = 1297339856
Address of id2 = 1297339860
Address of name = 1297339864
Address of c = 1297339865
Address of percentage = 1297339868
size of structure2 in bytes : 20
Address of id1 = 1297339824
Address of name = 1297339828
Address of id2 = 1297339832
Address of c = 1297339836
Address of percentage = 1297339840
```

Structure Padding Analysis for Above C Program

Memory Allocation for Structure1

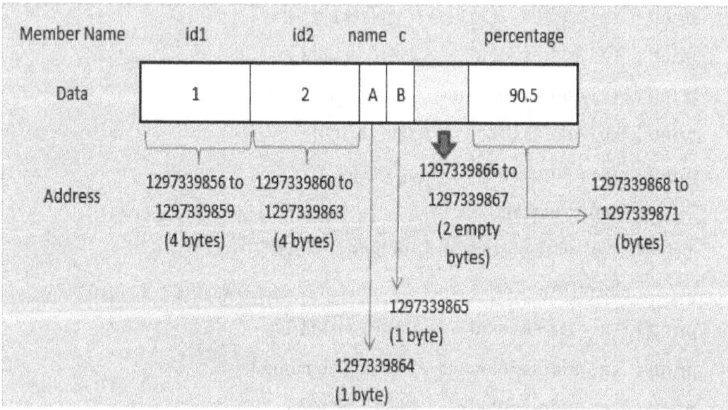

10.8. Unions

A **union** is a special data type available in C that allows to store different data types in the same memory location. You can define a union with many members, but only one member can contain a value at any given time. Unions provide an efficient way of using the same memory location for multiple-purpose.

Defining a Union

To define a union, you must use the **union** statement in the same way as you did while defining a structure. The union statement defines a new data type with more than one member for your program. The format of the union statement is as follows

```
union[union tag]{
  member definition;
  member definition;
...
  member definition;
}[one or more union variables];
```

The **union tag** is optional and each member definition is a normal variable definition, such as int i; or float f; or any other valid variable definition. At the end of the union's definition, before the final semicolon, you can specify one or more union variables but it is optional. Here is the way you would define a union type named Data having three members i, f, and str

```
unionData{
int i;
float f;
char str[20];
} data;
```

Now, a variable of **Data** type can store an integer, a floating-point number, or a string of characters. It means a single variable, i.e., same memory location, can be used to store multiple types of data. You can use any built-in or user defined data types inside a union based on your requirement.

The memory occupied by a union will be large enough to hold the largest member of the union. For example, in the above example, Data type will occupy 20 bytes of memory space because this is the maximum space which can be occupied by a character string. The following example displays the total memory size occupied by the above union –

```
#include<stdio.h>
#include<string.h>
unionData{
int i;
float f;
char str[20];
};
int main(){
unionData data;
  printf("Memory size occupied by data : %d\n",sizeof(data));
return0;
}
```

When the above code is compiled and executed, it produces the following result –

```
Memory size occupied by data : 20
```

Accessing Union Members

To access any member of a union, we use the **member access operator (.)**. The member access operator is coded as a period between the union variable name and the union member that we wish to access. You would use the keyword **union** to define variables of union type. The following example shows how to use unions in a program.

```
#include<stdio.h>
#include<string.h>
unionData{
int i;
float f;
char str[20];
};
int main(){
unionData data;
  data.i =10;
  data.f =220.5;
```

```
  strcpy( data.str,"C Programming");
  printf("data.i : %d\n", data.i);
  printf("data.f : %f\n", data.f);
  printf("data.str : %s\n", data.str);
return0;
}
```

When the above code is compiled and executed, it produces the following result.

```
data.i : 1917853763
data.f : 4122360580327794860452759994368.000000
data.str : C Programming
```

Here, we can see that the values of **i** and **f** members of union got corrupted because the final value assigned to the variable has occupied the memory location and this is the reason that the value of **str** member is getting printed very well.

Now let's look into the same example once again where we will use one variable at a time which is the main purpose of having unions.

```
#include<stdio.h>
#include<string.h>
unionData{
int i;
float f;
char str[20];
};
int main(){
unionData data;
  data.i =10;
  printf("data.i : %d\n", data.i);
  data.f =220.5;
  printf("data.f : %f\n", data.f);
  strcpy( data.str,"C Programming");
  printf("data.str : %s\n", data.str);
return0;
}
```

When the above code is compiled and executed, it produces the following result.

```
data.i : 10
data.f : 220.500000
data.str : C Programming
```

Here, all the members are getting printed very well because one member is being used at a time.

10.9. Structure vs Union

	Structure	Union
Memory Allocation	Members of structure do not share memory. So A structure need separate memory space for all its members i.e. all the members have unique storage.	A union shares the memory space among its members so no need to allocate memory to all the members. Shared memory space is allocated i.e. equivalent to the size of member having largest memory.
Member Access	Members of structure can be accessed individually at any time.	At a time, only one member of union can be accessed.
Keyword	To define Structure, '**struct**'keyword is used.	To define Union, '**union**'keyword is used.

10.10. Exercises

1) What will be the output of the C program?

```
#include<stdio.h>
int main()
{
        struct simp
        {
                int i = 6;
                char city[] = "chennai";
        };
        struct simp s1;
        printf("%d",s1.city);
        printf("%d", s1.i);
        return 0;
}
```

A. chennai 6

B. Nothing will be displayed

C. Runtime Error

D. Compilation Error

Answer

Option: D

Explanation

Compilation Error: Cannot initialize a class member here When we declared members in struture, it just tells the compiler about their presence. There is no memory allocated for that members. So we can't intialize structure members.

2) What will be the output of the C program?

```
#include<stdio.h>
struct
{
        int i;
        float ft;
}decl;
int main()
{
        decl.i = 4;
        decl.ft = 7.96623;
        printf("%d %.2f", decl.i, decl.ft);
        return 0;
}
```

A. 4 7.97

B. 4 7.96623

C. Compilation error

D. None of the above

Answer

Option: A

Explanation

In the above program the float variable ft is intialised to 7.96623, and it rounded of to 7.97 because of %.2f that we have mentioned in printf statement.

3) What will be the output of the C program?

```
#include<stdio.h>
int main()
{
        struct bitfields
        {
                int bits_1: 2;
                int bits_2: 4;
                int bits_3: 4;
                int bits_4: 3;
        }bit = {2, 3, 8, 7};
        printf("%d %d %d %d", bit.bits_1, bits.bit_2, bit.bits_3, bits.bit_4);
}
```

A. Runtime error

B. Compilation error

C. 2 3 8 7

D. -2 3 -8 -1

Answer

Option: D

Explanation

The above structure declaration shows that we declare four variables as int(whenever you declare int you get a signed int).

Signed integers needs the left most bit for +/- sign.

int bits_1: 2; // assigns two bits to the variable bits_1

int bits_2: 4; //assigns four bits to the variable bits_2

int bits_3: 4; //assigns four bits to the variable bits_3

int bits_4: 1; //assigns one bit to the variable bits_4

2 bits - 00

4 bits - 0000

1 bit - 0

We assign values 2, 3, 8, 1 for the variables bits_1, bits_2, bits_3 and bits_4 respectively.

When we assign 2 in 2 bit field:

Value bit

2 - 10

Here the left most bit is 1. so, the compiler treat the value as negative.

To handle negative values the system will use the 2's complement method.

1's complement of 2(10) - 01

2's complement of 2(10) - 10

Finally the value is -2.

When we assign 3 in 4 bit field:

Value bit

3 - 0011

Here the left most bit is 0. so, the compiler treat the value as positive.

There is no need of 2's complement. The compiler will displays 3.

When we assign 8 in 4-bit field:

Value bit

8 - 1000

here the left most bit is 1. so, the compiler treat the value as negative.

To handle negative values the system will use the 2's complement method.

1's complement of 8(1000) - 0111

2's complement of 8(1000) - 1000

Finally the value is -8.

when we assign 7 in 3-bit field:

value bit

7 - 111

here the left most bit is 1. so, the compiler treat the value as negative.

To handle negative values the system will use the 2's complement method.

1's complement of 7(111) - 000

2's complement of 7(111) - 001

Finally the value is -1.

4) What will be the output of the C program?

```
void main()
{
struct bitfields {
int bits_1: 2;
int bits_2: 9;
int bits_3: 6;
int bits_4: 1;
}bit;
```

```
printf("%d", sizeof(bit));
}
```

A. 2

B. 3

C. 4

D. 0

Answer

Option: B

Explanation

1 byte = 8 bits

In the above program we assign 2, 9, 6, 1 for the variables. Sum of the bits assigned is, 2 + 9 + 6 + 1 = 18, It is greater than 2 bytes, so it automatically takes 3 bytes.

5) What will be the output of the C program?

```
#include<stdio.h>
int main()
{
        struct leader
        {
        char *lead;
        int born;
        };
        struct leader l1 = {"AbdulKalam", 1931};
        struct leader l2 = l1;
        printf("%s %d", l2.lead, l1.born);
}
```

A. Compilation error

B. Garbage value 1931

C. AbdulKalam 1931

D. None of the above

Answer

Option: C

Explanation

We can assign one structure member to another structure member as like normal variable assign mentation. We can access the same values using different structure variables.

6) What will be the output of the C program?

```
#include<stdio.h>
struct employee
{
        char *empname;
        int salary;
};
int main()
{
        struct employee e, e1;
        e.empname = "Sridhar";
        e1 = e;
        printf("%s %s", e.empname, e1.empname);
        return 0;
}
```

A. Garbage value Sridhar

B. Sridhar Garbage value

C. Sridhar Sridhar

D. Compilation Error

Answer

Option: C

Explanation

We can assign structure variable to another structure variable and it can be accessed.

7) What will be the output of the C program (assume size of int as 2 bytes)?

```
#include<stdio.h>
int main()
{
        struct employee
        {
                int empid[5];
                int salary;
```

```
                employee *s;
        }emp;
printf("%d %d", sizeof(employee), sizeof(emp.empid));
return 0;
}
```

A. 6 2

B. 14 10

C. 8 2

D. 12 10

Answer

```
Option: B
```

Explanation

Structure always allocates memory for each of its members. Thats what happens here, an int occupies 2 bytes so empid variable occupies 10 bytes, variable salary occupies 2 bytes and the pointer variable occpies 2 bytes. So the sizeof structure employee occipes 14 bytes and structure member empid occupies 10 bytes.

8) What will be the output of the C program?

```
#include<stdio.h>
#include<string.h>
struct player
{
        char pname[20];
}pl;
char* play(struct player *temp_pl)
{
        strcpy(temp_pl->pname, "kohli");
        return temp_pl->pname;
}
int main()
{
        strcpy(pl.pname, "dhoni");
        printf("%s %s", pl.pname, play(&pl));
        return 0;
```

```
}
```

A. dhoni kohli

B. dhoni dhoni

C. None

D. kohli kohli

Answer

Option: D

Explanation

In the main function the string "dhoni" is copied to the structure member pl.pname using strcpy function(should have a prototype string.h). A function with structure member as a parameter play(&pl) - call by reference method, will be called inside the printf statement. The function is declared as, structure pointer temp_pl as a parameter and char pointer(which returns string) as a return type. Inside that function the string "kohli" is copied to the structure member temp_pl->pname, here temp_pl is the structure(player) variable and pname is the structure(player) member. So the new string is assinged to the structure member. Finally it will prints "kohli kohli".

9) What will be the output of the C program?

```
#include<stdio.h>
struct decl
{
        int n = 100;
}d1;
int main()
{
        printf("%d",d1.n);
        return 0;
}
```

A. 100

B. Compilation Error

C. 0

D. Garbage value

Answer

    Option: B

Explanation

Structure is used to declare a datatype, When we declare datatypes inside structure it does not allocate memory for it. So we can't store any data in a structure member.

10) What will be the output of the C program?

```
#include<stdio.h>
struct TeamScore
{
        int wickets;
        int score;
}ts = {2, 325};
struct country
{
        char *name;
}coun = {"India"};
int main()
{
        struct TeamScore tcon = ts;
        printf("%d %s %d", tcon.score, ts.wickets, coun.name);
        return 0;
}
```

A. 325 2 India

B. 325 2 garbage value

C. copilation error

D. None of the above

Answer

    Option: A

Explanation

The above program just prints all structure memeber values.

11) What will be the output of the C program?

```
#include<stdio.h>
int main()
```

```
{
        struct branch
        {
                char bran[10] = "Bangalore";
                int bpin = 431;
        };
        struct headoff
        {
                char head[10];
                int hpin;
        };
        struct headoff h = {"Chennai", 01};
        struct branch b;
        printf("HO - %s \n hpin - %d", h.head, h.hpin);
        printf("BO - %s \n bpin - %d", b.bran, b.bpin);
}
```

A. HO - Chennai hpin - 01 BO - Bangalore 431

B. HO - Chennai hpin - 01

C. Compilation Error

D. Runtime Error

Answer

Option: C

Explanation

Compilation Error: Cannot initialize a class member here.

12) What will be the output of the C program?

```
#include<stdio.h>
int main()
{
        struct str;
        {
                int s1;
                char st[30];
        };

        struct str s[] = { {1, "struct1"}, {2, "struct2"}, {3, "struct3"} };
```

```
        printf("%d %s", s[2].s1, (*(s+2)).st);
}
```

A. Compilation Error

B. 1 struct1

C. 2 struct2

D. 3 struct3

Answer

Option: D

Explanation

The above program has a structure str which has two members s1, st. The structure variable has been declared as array. So we can store multiple records in a structure. The printf statement which prints the corresponding records with respect to variables given in that statement.

Try By Yourself

1) What will be the output of the C program?

```
#include<stdio.h>
int main()
{
        struct play
        {
                char name[10];
                int playnum;
        };
        struct play p1 = {"virat", 18};
        struct play p2 = p1;
        if(p1 == p2)
        printf("Two structure members are equal");
        return 0;
}
```

A. Compilation Error

B. Two structure members are equal

C. Nothing will be display

D. Runtime Error

2) What will be the output of the C program?

```
#include<stdio.h>
int main()
{
        enum numbers{num1 = 1.5, num2 = 0, num3, num4, num5, num6}n;
        printf("%d %d\n", num1, num2);
}
```

A. 1.5 0

B. 1.5 2

C. 1.5 2.5

D. Compilation Error

3) What will be the output of the C program?

```
#include<stdio.h>
int main()
{
        struct alphabets
        {
                char firstLetter;
                struct alphabets a;
        }al;
        al.firstLetter = 'a';
        printf("%c", al.firstLetter);
}
```

A. a

B. Linker Error

C. Runtime Error

D. Compilation Error

4) What will be the output of the C program?

```
#include<stdio.h>
int main()
{
        struct check
        {
        }ck;
        printf("%d", sizeof(ck));
}
```

A. 0

B. 1

C. 2

D. Compilation Error

E. None

5) What will be the output of the C program?

```
#include<stdio.h>
int main()
{
        struct check
        {
        int i:0;
        }ck;
        printf("%d", sizeof(ck));
}
```

A. 0

B. 2

C. Compilation Error

D. 4

6) What will be the output of the C program?

```
#include<stdio.h>
int main()
{
        struct num
        {
        int i, j, k, l;
        };
        struct num n = {1, 2, 3};
        printf("%d %d %d %d", n.i, n.j, n.k, n.l);
}
```

A. 1 2 3 garbage value

B. 1 2 3 0

C. 1 2 3 3

D. None of the above

Answer

1) a 2)d 3)d 4)b 5)c 6)b

CHAPTER 11

FILE INPUT/OUTPUT

11.1. Introduction

A **file** represents a sequence of bytes on the disk where a group of related data is stored. File is created for permanent storage of data. It is a ready made structure.

In C language, we use a structure **pointer of file type** to declare a file.

FILE *fp;

11.2. File Operations

C provides a number of functions that helps to perform basic file operations. Following are the functions.

Function	description
fopen()	create a new file or open a existing file
fclose()	closes a file
getc()	reads a character from a file
putc()	writes a character to a file
fscanf()	reads a set of data from a file
fprintf()	writes a set of data to a file
getw()	reads a integer from a file
putw()	writes a integer to a file
fseek()	set the position to desire point
ftell()	gives current position in the file
rewind()	set the position to the begining point

11.3. Opening a File or Creating a File

The fopen() function is used to create a new file or to open an existing file.

General Syntax

*fp = FILE *fopen(const char *filename, const char *mode);

Here, *fp is the FILE pointer (FILE *fp), which will hold the reference to the opened(or created) file.

filename is the name of the file to be opened and **mode** specifies the purpose of opening the file. Mode can be of following types:

mode	Description
r	opens a text file in reading mode
w	opens or create a text file in writing mode.
a	opens a text file in append mode
r+	opens a text file in both reading and writing mode
w+	opens a text file in both reading and writing mode
a+	opens a text file in both reading and writing mode
rb	opens a binary file in reading mode
wb	opens or create a binary file in writing mode
ab	opens a binary file in append mode
rb+	opens a binary file in both reading and writing mode
wb+	opens a binary file in both reading and writing mode
ab+	opens a binary file in both reading and writing mode

Closing a File

The fclose() function is used to close an already opened file.

General Syntax

```
int fclose( FILE *fp);
```

Here fclose() function closes the file and returns **zero** on success, or **EOF** if there is an error in closing the file. This **EOF** is a constant defined in the header file **stdio.h**.

Input/Output Operation on File

In the above table we have discussed about various file I/O functions to perform reading and writing on file. getc() and putc() are the simplest functions which can be used to read and write individual characters to a file.

```
#include<stdio.h>
int main()
{
  FILE *fp;
  char ch;
  fp =fopen("one.txt","w");
printf("Enter data...");
while((ch =getchar())!= EOF){
putc(ch, fp);
}
fclose(fp);
  fp =fopen("one.txt","r");
```

```
while((ch =getc(fp)!= EOF)
printf("%c",ch);
// closing the file pointer
fclose(fp);
return0;
}
```

Reading and Writing to File Using fprintf() and fscanf()

```
#include<stdio.h>
struct emp
{
   char name[10];
   int age;
};
void main()
{
   struct emp e;
   FILE *p,*q;
   p =fopen("one.txt","a");
   q =fopen("one.txt","r");
printf("Enter Name and Age:");
scanf("%s %d", e.name,&e.age);
fprintf(p,"%s %d", e.name, e.age);
fclose(p);
do
{
fscanf(q,"%s %d", e.name, e.age);
printf("%s %d", e.name, e.age);
}
while(!feof(q));
}
```

In this program, we have created two FILE pointers and both are refering to the same file but in different modes. fprintf() function directly writes into the file, while fscanf() reads from the file, which can then be printed on the console using standard printf() function.

11.4. Difference between Append and Write Mode

Write (w) mode and Append (a) mode, while opening a file are almost the same. Both are used to write in a file. In both the modes, new file is created if it doesn't exists already.

The only difference they have is, when you **open** a file in the **write** mode, the file is reset, resulting in deletion of any data already present in the file. While in **append** mode this will not happen.

Append mode is used to append or add data to the existing data of file(if any). Hence, when you open a file in Append(a) mode, the cursor is positioned at the end of the present data in the file.

Reading and Writing in a Binary File

A Binary file is similar to a text file, but it contains only large numerical data. The Opening modes are mentioned in the table for opening modes above.

fread() and fwrite() functions are used to read and write is a binary file.

fwrite(data-element-to-be-written, size_of_elements, number_of_elements, pointer-to-file);

fread() is also used in the same way, with the same arguments like fwrite() function.

Below mentioned is a simple example of writing into a binary file

```
const char *mytext ="The quick brown fox jumps over the lazy dog";
FILE *bfp=fopen("test.txt","wb");
if(bfp)
{
fwrite(mytext,sizeof(char),strlen(mytext), bfp);
fclose(bfp);
}
```

11.5. Random Access To File

There is no need to read each record sequentially, if we want to access a particular record.C supports these functions for random access file processing.

1. fseek()
2. ftell()
3. rewind()

fseek()

This function is used for seeking the pointer position in the file at the specified byte.

Syntax: fseek(file pointer, displacement, pointer position);

Where

file pointer ---- It is the pointer which points to the file.

displacement ---- It is positive or negative.This is the number of bytes which are skipped backward (if negative) or forward(if positive) from the current position.This is attached with L because this is a long integer.

Pointer Position

This sets the pointer position in the file.

Value	pointer position
0	Beginning of file.
1	Current position
2	End of file

1). fseek(p,10L,0)

0 means pointer position is on beginning of the file,from this statement pointer position is skipped 10 bytes from the beginning of the file.

2). fseek(p,5L,1)

1 means current position of the pointer position.From this statement pointer position is skipped 5 bytes forward from the current position.

3). fseek(p,-5L,1)

From this statement pointer position is skipped 5 bytes backward from the current position.

ftell()

This function returns the value of the current pointer position in the file.The value is count from the beginning of the file.

Syntax

```
ftell(fptr);
```

Where fptr is a file pointer.

rewind()

This function is used to move the file pointer to the beginning of the given file.

Syntax

```
rewind( fptr);
```

Where fptr is a file pointer.

Example program for fseek()

Write a program to read last 'n' characters of the file using appropriate file functions(Here we need fseek() and fgetc()).

```
#include<stdio.h>
#include<conio.h>
void main()
{
   FILE *fp;
   char ch;
   clrscr();
   fp=fopen("file1.c", "r");
   if(fp==NULL)
              printf("file cannot be opened");
   else
   {
                          printf("Enter value of n  to read last 'n' characters");
                          scanf("%d",&n);
                          fseek(fp,-n,2);
                          while((ch=fgetc(fp))!=EOF)
                          {
                           printf("%c\t",ch);
                          }
   }
              fclose(fp);
              getch();
}
```

Output

It depends on the content in the file.

11.6. Preprocessors

The **C Preprocessor** is not a part of the compiler, but is a separate step in the compilation process. In simple terms, a C Preprocessor is just a text substitution tool and it instructs the compiler to do required pre-processing before the actual compilation. We'll refer to the C Preprocessor as CPP. All preprocessor commands begin with a hash symbol (#). It must be the first nonblank character, and for readability, a preprocessor directive should begin in the first column. The following section lists down all the important preprocessor directives

Sr.No.	Directive & Description
1	**#define** Substitutes a preprocessor macro.
2	**#include** Inserts a particular header from another file.
3	**#undef** Undefines a preprocessor macro.
4	**#ifdef** Returns true if this macro is defined.
5	**#ifndef** Returns true if this macro is not defined.
6	**#if** Tests if a compile time condition is true.
7	**#else** The alternative for #if.
8	**#elif** #else and #if in one statement.
9	**#endif** Ends preprocessor conditional.
10	**#error** Prints error message on stderr.
11	**#pragma** Issues special commands to the compiler, using a standardized method.

Preprocessors Examples

Analyze the following examples to understand various directives.

```
#define MAX_ARRAY_LENGTH 20
```

This directive tells the CPP to replace instances of MAX_ARRAY_LENGTH with 20. Use *#define* for constants to increase readability.

```
#include<stdio.h>
#include"myheader.h"
```

These directives tell the CPP to get stdio.h from **System Libraries** and add the text to the current source file. The next line tells CPP to get **myheader.h**from the local directory and add the content to the current source file.

```
#undef  FILE_SIZE
#define FILE_SIZE 42
```

It tells the CPP to undefine existing FILE_SIZE and define it as 42.

```
#ifndef MESSAGE
#define MESSAGE "You wish!"
#endif
```

It tells the CPP to define MESSAGE only if MESSAGE isn't already defined.

```
#ifdef DEBUG
/* Your debugging statements here */
#endif
```

It tells the CPP to process the statements enclosed if DEBUG is defined. This is useful if you pass the *-DDEBUG* flag to the gcc compiler at the time of compilation. This will define DEBUG, so you can turn debugging on and off on the fly during compilation.

Predefined Macros

ANSI C defines a number of macros. Although each one is available for use in programming, the predefined macros should not be directly modified.

Sr.No.	Macro & Description
1	**__DATE__** The current date as a character literal in "MMM DD YYYY" format.
2	**__TIME__** The current time as a character literal in "HH:MM:SS" format.
3	**__FILE__** This contains the current filename as a string literal.
4	**__LINE__** This contains the current line number as a decimal constant.
5	**__STDC__** Defined as 1 when the compiler complies with the ANSI standard.

Let's try the following example.

```
#include<stdio.h>
int main(){
  printf("File :%s\n", __FILE__ );
  printf("Date :%s\n", __DATE__ );
  printf("Time :%s\n", __TIME__ );
  printf("Line :%d\n", __LINE__ );
  printf("ANSI :%d\n", __STDC__ );
}
```

When the above code in a file **test.c** is compiled and executed, it produces the following result.

```
File :test.c
Date :Jun 2 2012
Time :03:36:24
Line :8
ANSI :1
```

Preprocessor Operators

The C preprocessor offers the following operators to help create macros –

The Macro Continuation (\) Operator

A macro is normally confined to a single line. The macro continuation operator (\) is used to continue a macro that is too long for a single line. For example.

```
#define message_for(a, b) \
  printf(#a " and "#b ": We love you!\n")
```

The Stringize (#) Operator

The stringize or number-sign operator ('#'), when used within a macro definition, converts a macro parameter into a string constant. This operator may be used only in a macro having a specified argument or parameter list. For example –

```
#include<stdio.h>
#define message_for(a, b) \
  printf(#a " and "#b ": We love you!\n")
int main(void){
  message_for(Carole,Debra);
return0;
}
```

When the above code is compiled and executed, it produces the following result.

```
Carole and Debra: We love you!
```

The Token Pasting (##) Operator

The token-pasting operator (##) within a macro definition combines two arguments. It permits two separate tokens in the macro definition to be joined into a single token. For example.

```
#include<stdio.h>
#define tokenpaster(n) printf ("token"#n " = %d", token##n)
int main(void){
int token34 =40;
  tokenpaster(34);
return0;
}
```

When the above code is compiled and executed, it produces the following result –

```
token34 = 40
```

It happened so because this example results in the following actual output from the preprocessor.

```
printf ("token34 = %d", token34);
```

This example shows the concatenation of token##n into token34 and here we have used both **stringize** and **token-pasting**.

The Defined() Operator

The preprocessor **defined** operator is used in constant expressions to determine if an identifier is defined using #define. If the specified identifier is defined, the value is true (non-zero). If the symbol is not defined, the value is false (zero). The defined operator is specified as follows.

```
#include<stdio.h>
#if !defined (MESSAGE)
#define MESSAGE "You wish!"
#endif
int main(void){
  printf("Here is the message: %s\n", MESSAGE);
return0;
}
```

When the above code is compiled and executed, it produces the following result –

```
Here is the message: You wish!
```

Parameterized Macros

One of the powerful functions of the CPP is the ability to simulate functions using parameterized macros. For example, we might have some code to square a number as follows.

```
int square(int x){
return x * x;
}
```

We can rewrite above the code using a macro as follows.

```
#define square(x)((x)*(x))
```

Macros with arguments must be defined using the **#define** directive before they can be used. The argument list is enclosed in parentheses and must immediately follow the macro name. Spaces are not allowed between the macro name and open parenthesis. For example

```
#include<stdio.h>
#define MAX(x,y)((x)>(y)?(x):(y))
int main(void){
  printf("Max between 20 and 10 is %d\n", MAX(10,20));
return0;
}
```

When the above code is compiled and executed, it produces the following result.

```
Max between 20 and 10 is 20
```

11.7. Exercises

1) What will be the output of the C program?

```
#include<stdio.h>
int main()
{
        int EOF = 0;
        printf("%d", EOF);
        return 0;
}
```

A. -1

B. 0

C. 1

D. Compilation Error

Answer

Option: D

Explanation

In C, EOF is a predefined macro constant. we can't change the value of constant. So, it results into an error message.

2) What will be the output of the C program?

```
#include<stdio.h>
int main()
{
        printf("%d", EOF);
        return 0;
}
```

A. NULL

B. -1

C. 0

D. Compilation Error

Answer

Option: B

Explanation

In C, EOF - End of File which is a macro and its header file is stdio.h. In C, EOF is equal to -1 by default. We can use EOF in some programs to check whether file pointer reaches the end of the file

3) What will be the output of the C program?

```
#include<stdio.h>
int main() {
        EOF++;
        printf("%d", EOF);
        return 0;
}
```

A. Compilation Error

B. -1

C. 0

D. 1

Answer

Option: A

Explanation

In C, EOF is a predefined macro constant. we can't change the value of constant. So, it results into an error message.

4) What will be the output of the C program?

```
/*This program uses the datafile.txt which contains the following data*/
/* Hai. This is christuniversity.in */
#include<stdio.h>
int main()
{
        unsigned char ch;
        FILE *fp;
        fp = fopen("datafile.txt", "r");
        while ((ch = fgetc(fp)) != EOF)
        {
                printf("%c", ch);
        }
        printf(" Thank you.");
        fclose(fp);
        return 0;
}
```

A.Compilation Error

B.It will print nothing.

C."Hai. christuniversity.in. Thank you."

D."Hai. This is christuniversity.in " and loop continues for infinite times

Answer

Option: D

Explanation

The above C program opens a file(datafile.txt) in read mode. The program gives us a permisson to read data in that file. Here we get data using fgetc(fp) and stored it to the variable ch(unsigned char type), each time the loop checks whether the file pointer reaches the end of a file or not by using EOF(which is predefined macro in c). EOF is equivalent to -1 which is a non-zero value. So the loop executes for infinite times after reading that file data. You should notice that we have declared a unsigned char.

5) What will be the output of the C program?

```
/*This program uses the datafile.txt which contains the following data*/
/* Hai. This is christuniversity.in */
#include<stdio.h>
int main()
{
        char ch;
        FILE *fp;
        fp = fopen("datafile.txt", "w");
        while ((ch = fgetc(fp)) != EOF)
        {
                printf("%c", ch);
        }
        printf("Thank you.");
        fclose(fp);
        return 0;
}
```

A. Hai. This is christuniversity.in. Thank you.

B. Thank you.

C. Hai. This is christuniversity.in. and enters into an infinite loop.

D. Compilation Error.

Answer

Option: B

Explanation

In this program we have just changed that unsigned char to char data type and also the file mode to write "w". So when we try to read the file using fgetc(fp), it will not work. The control directly passes next statement("Thank you.") after the while loop. We have the permission to write a file so we can't read.

6) What will be the output of the C program?

```
/*This program uses two files*/
#include<stdio.h>
int main()
{
        char ch;
        FILE *fptr1, *fptr2;
        fp = fopen("datafile1.txt", "w");
        fp = fopen("datafile2.txt", "w");
        printf("Thank you.");
        fclose(*fptr1, *fptr2);
        return 0;
}
```

A. Thank you.

B. Prints nothing

C. Compilation error

D. None of the above

Answer

Option: C

Explanation

Error: too many arguments to function 'int fclose(FILE*)'. This error will appears if you run the above program. The fclose() function closes only one file at a time, we cannot close more than one file.

7) What will be the output of the C program?

```
#include<stdio.h>
int main()
{
        char *str = "CHRIST";
        while (*str)
        {
                putc(*str, stdout);
                fputchar(*str);
                printf("%c", *str);
```

```
                    str++;
            }
            return 0;
}
```

A. CHRIST

B. CCHHRRIISSTT

C. CCCHHHRRRIIISSSTTT

D. CHRIST CHRIST CHRIST

Answer

Option: C

Explanation

In the above C program, we have use three functions are all used for the same purpose(to print data in standard output screen). The putc() function is used to print a single character, the fputchar also used to print a single character in output screen and the printf statement is used to print a single character in a output screen.

8) What will be the output of the C program?

```
#include<stdio.h>
int main()
{
            int f1, f2;
            FILE *fp;
            fp = fopen("datafile.txt", "w");
            f1 = EOF;
            f2 = feof(fp);
            if(f1 == f2)
            {
                    printf("EOF and feof(), both returns the same value");
            }
            else
            {
                    printf("EOF and feof() both returns different values");
            }
            return 0;
}
```

A. Nothing will be displayed

B. EOF and feof() both returns the same value

C. EOF and feof() both returns different values

D. Runtime Error

Answer

Option: C

Explanation

EOF returns -1 and feof() function returns 0. So the else part is executed.

9) What will be the output of the C program?

```
/*This program uses the datafile.txt which contains the following data*/
/* Hai. This is 2braces.com. */
#include<stdio.h>
int main()
{
        char *str = "We are christuniversity.in";
        fprintf(stdout, str);
        return 0;
}
```

A. Compilation Error

B. Runtime Error

C. Linker Error

D. We are christuniversity.in

Answer

Option: D

Explanation

In C, stdout - standard output which is nothing but the output screen. In the above C program we had fprintf statement with two parameters(stdout and the variable name) which writes data into output screen.

10) What will be the output of the C program?

```
/*creating new file and writing data into a file*/
#include<stdio.h>
```

```
int main()
{
        FILE *fptr;
        char name[40], name1[40];
        fptr = fopen("record.txt", "r+");
        if(fptr == NULL)
        {
                printf("File not exist");
                exit(1);
        }
        printf("Enter your name: ");
        gets(name);
        fputs(name, fptr);
        rewind(fptr);
        fgets(name1, 40, fptr);
        printf("Name: %s", name1);
        fclose(fptr);
        return 0;
}
/*say you give a name john*/
```

A. File Not Exist

B. Name: John

C. Name: John garbage value

D. Compilation Error

Answer

Option: A

Explanation

In the above C program we opens a file in "r+" mode.

The "r+" mode doesnot create a new file.

It only reads and write into a file(if already exists). So the fopen() function returns NULL to the fptr and if condition block executed.

Try By Yourself

1) What will be the output of the C program?

```
/*The file datafile.txt is already exists.*/
/*This program uses the datafile.txt which contains the following data*/
/* Hai. This is google.com */
#include<stdio.h>
int main()
{
        char ch;
        FILE *fptr;
        fptr = fopen("datafile.txt", "w+");
        fclose(fptr);
        fptr = fopen("datafile.txt", "r");
        while((ch = fgetc(fptr))!= EOF)
        {
                printf("%c",ch);
        }
        fclose(fptr);
        return 0;
}
```

A. Hello

B. Garbage values

C. Compilation Error

D. Nothing will be displayed

2) What will be the output of the C program?

```
/*This program uses the file "int_numbers.txt"*/
/*4 5 6 5*/
#include<stdio.h>
int main()
{
        int num[4];
        int i = 0, tot = 0;
        FILE *fptr;
        fptr = fopen("int_numbers.txt", "r");
```

```
        if(fptr == NULL)
  {
                printf("File not exist");
  }
        for(i = 0; i < 4; i++)
  {
                fscanf(fptr, "%d,", &num[i]);
  }
        for(i = 0; i < 4; i++)
        {
                printf("%d ", num[i]);
                tot = tot + num[i];
        }
        printf("tot = %d", tot);
        fclose(fptr);
        return 0;
}
```

A. Compilation Error

B.4 5 6 tot = 15

C. 4 5 6 5

D. 4 5 6 5 tot = 20

3) What will be the output of the C program?

```
/*This program uses the file "float_num.txt"*/
/*1.5 2.6 3.7 4.8*/
#include<stdio.h>

int main()
{
        float num[4];
        float i = 0, tot = 0;
        FILE *fptr;
        fptr = fopen("float_num.txt", "r");
        if(fptr == NULL)
  {
```

```
                    printf("File not exist");
  }
            fclose(fptr);
            for(i = 0; i < 4; i++)
            {
                    fscanf(fptr, "%f", &num[i]);
            }
            for(i = 0; i < 4; i++)
            {
                    tot = tot + num[i];
            }
            printf("tot = %f", tot);
            return 0;
}
```

A. 12.60000

B. sum of garbage values

C. Compilation Error

D. Runtime Error

4) What will be the output of the C program?

```
/*This program uses the file "float_num1.txt"*/
/*1.5, 2.6, 3.7, 4.8*/
#include<stdio.h>
int main()
{
            float num[4];
            float i = 0, tot = 0;
            FILE *fptr;
            fptr = fopen("float_num1.txt", "r");
            if(fptr == NULL)
  {
                    printf("File not exist");
  }
            fclose(fptr);
            for(i = 0; i < 4; i++)
```

```
        {
                fscanf(fptr, "%f", &num[i]);
        }
        for(i = 0; i < 4; i++)
        {
                tot = tot + num[i];
        }
        printf("tot = %f", tot);
        return 0;
}
```

A. 12.600000

B. 12.000000

C. Null or Unexpected Result

D. Compilation Error

5) What will be the output of the C program?

```
#include<stdio.h>
int main()
{
        fprintf(&_streams[1], "This will display");
        return 0;
}
```

A. Prints nothing

B. This will display

C. Compilation Error

D. Linker Error

Answer

1)d 2)d 3)b 4)c 5)b

CHAPTER 12

GRAPHICS PROGRAMMING IN C

12.1. Introduction

This **chapter mainly** for those who want to learn fundamentals of Graphics programming, without any prior knowledge of graphics. This also contains lots of fundamental graphics program like drawing of various geometrical shapes(rectangle, circle eclipse etc), use of mathematical function in drawing curves, coloring an object with different colors and patterns and simple animation programs like jumping ball and moving cars. This tutorial will provide you an overview of computer graphics and it's fundamentals. The first step in any graphics program is to initialize the graphics drivers on the computer using **initgraph** method of graphics.h library.

void initgraph(int *graphicsDriver, int *graphicsMode, char *driverDirectoryPath);

It initializes the graphics system by loading the passed graphics driver then changing the system into graphics mode. It also resets or initializes all graphics settings like color, palette, current position etc, to their default values. Below is the description of input parameters of initgraph function.

- **graphicsDriver** : It is a pointer to an integer specifying the graphics driver to be used. It tells the compiler that what graphics driver to use or to automatically detect the drive. In all our programs we will use **DETECT** macro of graphics.h library that instruct compiler for auto detection of graphics driver.
- **graphicsMode** : It is a pointer to an integer that specifies the graphics mode to be used. If *graphdriver is set to DETECT, then initgraph sets *graphmode to the highest resolution available for the detected driver.
- **driverDirectoryPath** : It specifies the directory path where graphics driver files (BGI files) are located. If directory path is not provided, then it will seach for driver files in current working directory directory. In all our sample graphics programs, you have to change path of BGI directory accordingly where you turbo C compiler is installed.

12.2. Colors in C Graphics Programming

There are 16 colors declared in C Graphics. We use colors to set the current drawing color, change the color of background, change the color of text, to color a closed shape etc. To specify a color, we can either use color constants like setcolor(RED), or their corresponding integer codes like setcolor(4). Below is the color code in increasing order.

COLOR MACRO	INTEGER VALUE
BLACK	0
BLUE	1
GREEN	2
CYAN	3
RED	4
MAGENTA	5
BROWN	6
LIGHTGRAY	7
DARKGRAY	8
LIGHTBLUE	9
LIGHTGREEN	10
LIGHTCYAN	11
LIGHTRED	12
LIGHTMAGENTA	13
YELLOW	14
WHITE	15

At the end of our graphics program, we have to unloads the graphics drivers and sets the screen back to text mode by calling **closegraph** function. Here is our first C Graphics program to draw a straight line on screen.

```
/* C graphics program to draw a line */
#include<graphics.h>
#include<conio.h>
int main() {
  int gd = DETECT, gm;
  /* initialization of graphic mode */
  initgraph(&gd, &gm, "C:\\TC\\BGI");
  line(100,100,200, 200);
  getch();
  closegraph();
  return 0;
}
```

In this program **initgraph** function auto detects an appropriate graphics driver and sets graphics mode maximum possible screen resolution. Then **line** function draws a straight line from coordinate (100, 100) to (200, 200). Then we added a call to getch function to avoid instant termination of program as it waits for user to press any key. At last, we unloads the graphics drivers and sets the screen back to text mode by calling **closegraph** function.

12.3. Sample Graphics Program in C

1. *Draw Shapes Using c Graphics*

This c graphics program draws basic shapes such as circle, line, rectangle, ellipse and display text on screen using c graphics. This can be a first graphics program for a beginner.

C Programming Code

```
#include<graphics.h>
#include<conio.h>
main()
{
  int gd = DETECT,gm,left=100,top=100,right=200,bottom=200,x=
300,y=150,radius=50;
   initgraph(&gd, &gm, "C:\\TC\\BGI");
   rectangle(left, top, right, bottom);
  circle(x, y, radius);
  bar(left + 300, top, right + 300, bottom);
  line(left - 10, top + 150, left + 410, top + 150);
  ellipse(x, y + 200, 0, 360, 100, 50);
  outtextxy(left + 100, top + 325, "My First C Graphics Program");
   getch();
  closegraph();
  return 0;
}
```

2. *C program Draw Bar Chart*

This program draws bar chart using c graphics. Chart is drawn using bars filled with different styles and in different colors.

C Programming Code

```
#include <graphics.h>
#include <conio.h>
main()
{
  int gd = DETECT, gm;
   initgraph(&gd, &gm, "C:\\TC\\BGI");
```

```
setcolor(YELLOW);
rectangle(0,30,639,450);
settextstyle(SANS_SERIF_FONT,HORIZ_DIR,2);
setcolor(WHITE);
outtextxy(275,0,"Bar Chart");
setlinestyle(SOLID_LINE,0,2);
line(100,420,100,60);
line(100,420,600,420);
line(90,70,100,60);
line(110,70,100,60);
line(590,410,600,420);
line(590,430,600,420);
outtextxy(95,35,"Y");
outtextxy(610,405,"X");
outtextxy(85,415,"O");
setfillstyle(LINE_FILL,BLUE);
bar(150,100,200,419);
setfillstyle(XHATCH_FILL,RED);
bar(225,150,275,419);
setfillstyle(WIDE_DOT_FILL,GREEN);
bar(300,200,350,419);
setfillstyle(INTERLEAVE_FILL,MAGENTA);
bar(375,125,425,419);
setfillstyle(HATCH_FILL,BROWN);
bar(450,175,500,419);
getch();
return 0;
}
```

3. *C Program to Draw Pie Chart*

C Programming Code

```
/* Program to draw a pie chart */
#include<graphics.h>
#include<conio.h>
int main()
{
  int gd = DETECT, gm, midx, midy;
  initgraph(&gd, &gm, "C:\\TC\\BGI");
```

```
 setcolor(MAGENTA);
rectangle(0,40,639,450);
settextstyle(SANS_SERIF_FONT,HORIZ_DIR,2);
setcolor(WHITE);
outtextxy(275,10,"Pie Chart");
 midx = getmaxx()/2;
midy = getmaxy()/2;
 setfillstyle(LINE_FILL,BLUE);
pieslice(midx, midy, 0, 75, 100);
outtextxy(midx+100, midy - 75, "20.83%");
 setfillstyle(XHATCH_FILL,RED);
pieslice(midx, midy, 75, 225, 100);
outtextxy(midx-175, midy - 75, "41.67%");
 setfillstyle(WIDE_DOT_FILL,GREEN);
pieslice(midx, midy, 225, 360, 100);
outtextxy(midx+75, midy + 75, "37.50%");
 getch();
return 0;
}
```

4. *C Program to Move a Car*

Program in c using graphics move a car. A car is made using two rectangles and two circles which act as tyres of car. A for loop is used to move the car forward by changing the rectangle and circle coordinates and erasing the previous contents on screen using clearviewport, you can also use cleardevice. Speed of car can be adjusted using delay function, more the delay lesser will be the speed or lesser the delay your car will move fast. In this program color of the car also keeps on changing, this is accomplished by incrementing the color value by one each time in for loop, you can also use random function for this purpose. Before you see a car moving you will be asked to press a key.

C Programming Code

```
#include <graphics.h>
#include <dos.h>
#include <conio.h>
 main()
```

```
{
  int i, j = 0, gd = DETECT, gm;
   initgraph(&gd,&gm,"C:\\TC\\BGI");
   settextstyle(DEFAULT_FONT,HORIZ_DIR,2);
  outtextxy(25,240,"Press any key to view the moving car");
   getch();
  setviewport(0,0,639,440,1);
   for( i = 0 ; i <= 420 ; i = i + 10, j++ )
  {
    rectangle(50+i,275,150+i,400);
    rectangle(150+i,350,200+i,400);
    circle(75+i,410,10);
    circle(175+i,410,10);
    setcolor(j);
    delay(100);
     if( i == 420 )
break;
     clearviewport();
  }
   getch();
  closegraph();
  return 0;
}
```

5. C Program to Draw a 3d Bar Chart

This c program draws a 3d bar chart.

C Programming Code

```
#include <graphics.h>
#include <conio.h>
 int main()
{
  int gd = DETECT, gm;
   initgraph(&gd, &gm, "C:\\TC\\BGI");
   setcolor(YELLOW);
```

```
rectangle(0,30,639,450);
settextstyle(SANS_SERIF_FONT,HORIZ_DIR,2);
setcolor(WHITE);
outtextxy(275,0,"Bar Chart");
setlinestyle(SOLID_LINE,0,2);
line(100,420,100,60);
line(100,420,600,420);
line(90,70,100,60);
line(110,70,100,60);
line(590,410,600,420);
line(590,430,600,420);
outtextxy(95,35,"Y");
outtextxy(610,405,"X");
outtextxy(85,415,"O");
setfillstyle(LINE_FILL,BLUE);
bar(150,100,200,419);
setfillstyle(XHATCH_FILL,RED);
bar(225,150,275,419);
setfillstyle(WIDE_DOT_FILL,GREEN);
bar(300,200,350,419);
setfillstyle(INTERLEAVE_FILL,MAGENTA);
bar(375,125,425,419);
setfillstyle(HATCH_FILL,BROWN);
bar(450,175,500,419);
getch();
return 0;
}
```

6. C Smiling Face Animation

This animation using C draws a smiling face which appears at random positions on the screen.

C Programming Code

```
#include<graphics.h>
#include<conio.h>
```

```
#include<stdlib.h>
main()
{
  int gd = DETECT, gm, area, temp1, temp2, left = 25, top = 75;
  void *p;
  initgraph(&gd, &gm, "C:\\TC\\BGI");
  setcolor(YELLOW);
  circle(50, 100, 25);
  setfillstyle(SOLID_FILL, YELLOW);
  floodfill(50, 100, YELLOW);
  setcolor(BLACK);
  setfillstyle(SOLID_FILL, BLACK);
  fillellipse(44, 85, 2, 6);
  fillellipse(56, 85, 2, 6);
  ellipse(50, 100, 205, 335, 20, 9);
  ellipse(50, 100, 205, 335, 20, 10);
  ellipse(50, 100, 205, 335, 20, 11);
  area = imagesize(left, top, left + 50, top + 50);
  p = malloc(area);
  setcolor(WHITE);
  settextstyle(SANS_SERIF_FONT, HORIZ_DIR, 2);
  outtextxy(155, 451, "Smiling Face Animation");
  setcolor(BLUE);
  rectangle(0, 0, 639, 449);
  while(!kbhit())
  {
    temp1 = 1 + random (588);
    temp2 = 1 + random (380);
    getimage(left, top, left + 50, top + 50, p);
    putimage(left, top, p, XOR_PUT);
    putimage(temp1 , temp2, p, XOR_PUT);
    delay(100);
    left = temp1;
    top = temp2;
```

```
    }
     getch();
    closegraph();
    return 0;
}
```

7. *Captcha Program in c*

This program generates captcha, a captcha is a random code generated using some algorithm. We will use random function in our code. These are used in typing tutors and in website to check whether a human is operating on a website.

C Programming Code

```
#include<stdlib.h>
#include<dos.h>
#include<graphics.h>
 main()
{
  int i = 0, key, num, midx, gd = DETECT, gm;
  char a[10];
   initgraph(&gd,&gm,"C:\\TC\\BGI");
   midx = getmaxx()/2;
   settextstyle(SCRIPT_FONT,HORIZ_DIR,5);
  settextjustify(CENTER_TEXT,CENTER_TEXT);
  setcolor(GREEN);
  outtextxy(midx,20,"CAPTCHA");
  settextstyle(SCRIPT_FONT,HORIZ_DIR,2);
  outtextxy(midx,125,"Press any key to change the generated random code
\"captcha\"");
  outtextxy(midx,150,"Press escape key to exit...");
   setcolor(WHITE);
  setviewport(100,200,600,400,1);
  setcolor(RED);
  randomize();
   while(1)
  {
```

```
    while(i<6)
    {
      num = random(3);
       if ( num == 0 )
         a[i] = 65 + random(26);   /* 65 is the ASCII value of A */
      else if ( num == 1)
         a[i] = 97 + random(26);   /* 97 is the ASCII value of a */
      else
         a[i] = 48 + random(10);   /* 48 is the ASCII value of 0 */
      i++;
    }
    a[i] = '\0';
    outtextxy(210,100,a);
    key = getch();
     if( key == 27 )             /* escape key*/
      exit(0);
    clearviewport();
    i = 0;
  }
}
```

12.4. Tricky Questions in C Programming (Interview Questions from TCS, CTS, ZOHO, etc.)

1) To check if two numbers are equal without using arithmetic operators or comparison operators.

The simplest solution for this is using Bitwise XOR operator (^). We know that, for two equal numbers XOR operator returns 0. We will use this trick to solve this problem.

```
// C program to check if two numbers are equal
// without using arithmetic operators or
// comparison operators
#include<stdio.h>
 int main()
{
  int x = 10;
```

```
    int y = 10;
    if ( !(x ^ y) )
      printf(" x is equal to y ");
    else
      printf(" x is not equal to y ");
    return 0;
  }
```

2) Program to find Maximum and minimum of two numbers without using any loop or condition.

   The simplest trick is,

```
// CPP program to find maximum and minimum of
// two numbers without using loop and any
// condition.
#include<bits/stdc++.h>
int main ()
{
  int a = 15, b = 20;
  printf("max = %d\n", ((a + b) + abs(a - b)) / 2);
  printf("min = %d", ((a + b) - abs(a - b)) / 2);
  return 0;
}
```

3) Odd or even program in C using modulus operator

Method 1

```
#include <stdio.h>
int main()
{
  int n;
  printf("Input an integer\n");
  scanf("%d", &n);
  if (n & 1 == 1)
    printf("Odd\n");
  else
    printf("Even\n");
  return 0;
}
```

Method 2

```
#include <stdio.h>
int main()
{
  int n;
  printf("Enter an integer\n");
  scanf("%d", &n);
  if ((n/2)*2 == n)
    printf("Even\n");
  else
    printf("Odd\n");
  return 0;
}
```

Method 3 (Without Using Conditional Statement)

```
#include<stdio.h>
int main()
{
  char arr[2][5] = {"Even", "Odd"};
  int no;
  printf( "Enter a number: ");
  scanf("%d",&no);
  printf("%d",arr[no%2]);
  getch();
  return 0;
}
```

4) Write a C program to swap two numbers without using third temp variable.

```
#include<stdio.h>
int main() {
  int num1, num2;
  printf("\nEnter First Number : ");
  scanf("%d", &num1);
  printf("\nEnter Second Number : ");
  scanf("%d", &num2);
  num1 = num1 ^ num2;
```

```
    num2 = num1 ^ num2;
    num1 = num1 ^ num2;
    printf("\n Numbers after Exchange : ");
    printf("\n Num1 = %d and Num2 = %d", num1, num2);
    return(0);
}
```

5) C program to run method before main method

```
#include<stdio.h>
/* Apply the constructor attribute to myStartupFun() so that it
   is executed before main() */
void myStartupFun (void) __attribute__ ((constructor));
/* Apply the destructor attribute to myCleanupFun() so that it
   is executed after main() */
void myCleanupFun (void) __attribute__ ((destructor));
/* implementation of myStartupFun */
void myStartupFun (void)
{
    printf ("startup code before main()\n");
}
/* implementation of myCleanupFun */
void myCleanupFun (void)
{
    printf ("cleanup code after main()\n");
}
int main (void)
{
    printf ("hello\n");
    return 0;
}
```

6) How do you print the format specifier like %d in C programming and what is the logic behind this?

```
int main()
{
printf("%%d");
return 0;
}
```

7) Write a C program which run without main() function

```
#include<stdio.h>
#define fun main
int fun(void)
{
  printf("Hello");
  return 0;
}
```

8) Create a Program which produce output "Hello World" , the program must not contains semicolon

Solution 1

```
#include<stdio.h>
void main(){
  if(printf("Hello world")){
  }
}
```

Solution 2

```
#include<stdio.h>
void main(){
  while(!printf("Hello world")){
  }
}
```

Solution 3

```
#include<stdio.h>
void main(){
  switch(printf("Hello world")){
  }
}
```

9) Write a c program to subtract two numbers without using subtraction operator

Solution 1

```
#include<stdio.h>
int main()
{
    int a, b, count = 0, temp;
    printf("\nEnter First Number:\t");
    scanf("%d", &a);
    printf("\nEnter Second Number:\t");
    scanf("%d", &b);
    temp = a;
    while(count < b)
    {
        a--;
        count++;
    }
    printf("\nSubtraction of Two Numbers %d and %d:\t%d\n", temp, b, a);
    return 0;
}
```

Solution 2

```
#include<stdio.h>
int main()
{
    int a, b, num1, num2;
    printf("\nEnter First Number:\t");
    scanf("%d", &a);
    printf("\nEnter Second Number:\t");
    scanf("%d", &b);
    num1 = a;
    num2 = b;
    while (b != 0)
    {
```

```
        int borrow = (~a) & b;
        a = a ^ b;
        b = borrow << 1;
    }
    printf("\nSubtraction of Two Numbers %d and %d:\t%d\n", num1, num2, a);
    return 0;
}
```

10) Write a scanf function in c which accept paragraph from user.

```
#include<stdio.h>
#define MAX 500
int main(){
  char arr[MAX];
  printf("Enter any paragraph which can include spaces or new line.\n");
  printf("To exit press the tab key.\n");
  scanf("%[^\t]s",arr);
  printf("You had entered: \n");
  printf("%s",arr);
  return 0;
}
```